Australian BUSH PUBS

A CELEBRATION OF OUTBACK AUSTRALIA'S ICONIC WATERING HOLES

Australian BUSH PUBS

A CELEBRATION OF OUTBACK AUSTRALIA'S ICONIC WATERING HOLES

CRAIG LEWIS & CATHY SAVAGE

www.woodslanepress.com.au

This book is for all, both past and present, who have stood at the bar of one of Australia's greatest outback institutions — the bush pub.

CONTENTS

Pub Locations Map	8-9
Introduction	11
Adavale Pub — Adavale QLD	14
Adelaide River Inn — Adelaide River NT	18
Albert Hotel — Milparinka NSW	22
Barrow Creek Hotel — Barrow Creek NT	26
Betoota Hotel — Betoota QLD	30
Birdsville Hotel — Birdsville QLD	34
Blue Heeler Hotel — Kynuna QLD	40
Broad Arrow Tavern — Broad Arrow WA	46
Cameron Corner Store — Cameron Corner QLD	50
Commercial Hotel — Bendoc VIC	56
Daly Waters Pub — Daly Waters NT	60
Dargo Hotel — Dargo VIC	66
Einasleigh Hotel — Einasleigh QLD	68
Gladstone Hotel — Wyandra QLD	74
Glengarry Hilton — Glengarry NSW	78
Grand Hotel — Kookynie WA	82
Gregory Downs Hotel — Gregory Downs QLD	86
Hebel Hotel — Hebel QLD	90
Homebush Hotel — Penarie NSW	96
Imperial Hotel — Ravenswood QLD	102
Innamincka Hotel — Innamincka SA	106
Ironclad Hotel — Marble Bar WA	110
Jennacubbine Tavern — Jennacubbine WA	114
Kevington Hotel — Kevington VIC	118
Kingoonya Hotel — Kingoonya SA	122
Larrimah Hotel — Larrimah NT	128
Lions Den Hotel — Helenvale QLD	132
Marree Hotel — Marree SA	136
Middleton Hotel — Middleton QLD	140
Mingela Hotel — Mingela QLD	146
Nerriga Hotel — Nerriga NSW	150
Nindigully Pub — Nindigully QLD	154
Noccundra Hotel — Noccundra QLD	160
Oasis Roadhouse — The Lynd Junction QLD	166
Overland Corner Hotel — Overland Corner SA	170
Prairie Hotel — Prairie QLD	176
Royal Hotel — Bedourie QLD	182
Royal Hotel — Eromanga QLD	186
Royal Mail Hotel — Hungerford QLD	188
Silverton Hotel — Silverton NSW	194
Sofala Royal Hotel — Sofala NSW	198
South Western Hotel — Toompine QLD	202
Surveyor General Inn — Berrima NSW	208
The Dangi Pub — Urandangi QLD	212
The Family Hotel — Tibooburra NSW	218
The Logan Pub — Logan VIC	222
The Pub in the Paddock — Pyengana TAS	226
Tilpa Hotel — Tilpa NSW	232
Warrego Hotel — Fords Bridge NSW	236
William Creek Hotel — William Creek SA	240
Yaraka Hotel — Yaraka QLD	246
Index	250
About the Authors	255

PUB LOCATIONS

1	Adavale Pub — QLD		18	Hebel Hotel — QLD		35	Overland Corner Hotel — SA
2	Adelaide River Inn — NT		19	Homebush Hotel — NSW		36	Prairie Hotel — QLD
3	Albert Hotel — NSW		20	Imperial Hotel — QLD		37	Royal Hotel — Bedourie QLD
4	Barrow Creek Hotel — NT		21	Innamincka Hotel — SA		38	Royal Hotel — Eromanga QLD
5	Betoota Hotel — QLD		22	Ironclad Hotel — WA		39	Royal Mail Hotel — QLD
6	Birdsville Hotel — QLD		23	Jennacubbine Tavern — WA		40	Silverton Hotel — NSW
7	Blue Heeler Hotel — QLD		24	Kevington Hotel — VIC		41	Sofala Royal Hotel — NSW
8	Broad Arrow Tavern — WA		25	Kingoonya Pub — SA		42	South Western Hotel — QLD
9	Cameron Corner Store — QLD		26	Larrimah Hotel — NT		43	Surveyor General Inn — NSW
10	Commercial Hotel — VIC		27	Lions Den Hotel — QLD		44	The Dangi Pub — QLD
11	Daly Waters Pub — NT		28	Marree Hotel — SA		45	The Family Hotel — NSW
12	Dargo Hotel — VIC		29	Middleton Hotel — QLD		46	The Logan Pub — VIC
13	Einasleigh Hotel — QLD		30	Mingela Hotel — QLD		47	The Pub in the Paddock — TAS
14	Gladstone Hotel — QLD		31	Nerriga Hotel — NSW		48	Tilpa Hotel — NSW
15	Glengarry Hilton — NSW		32	Nindigully Pub — QLD		49	Warrego Hotel — NSW
16	Grand Hotel — WA		33	Noccundra Hotel — QLD		50	William Creek Hotel — SA
17	Gregory Downs Hotel — QLD		34	Oasis Roadhouse — QLD		51	Yaraka Hotel — QLD

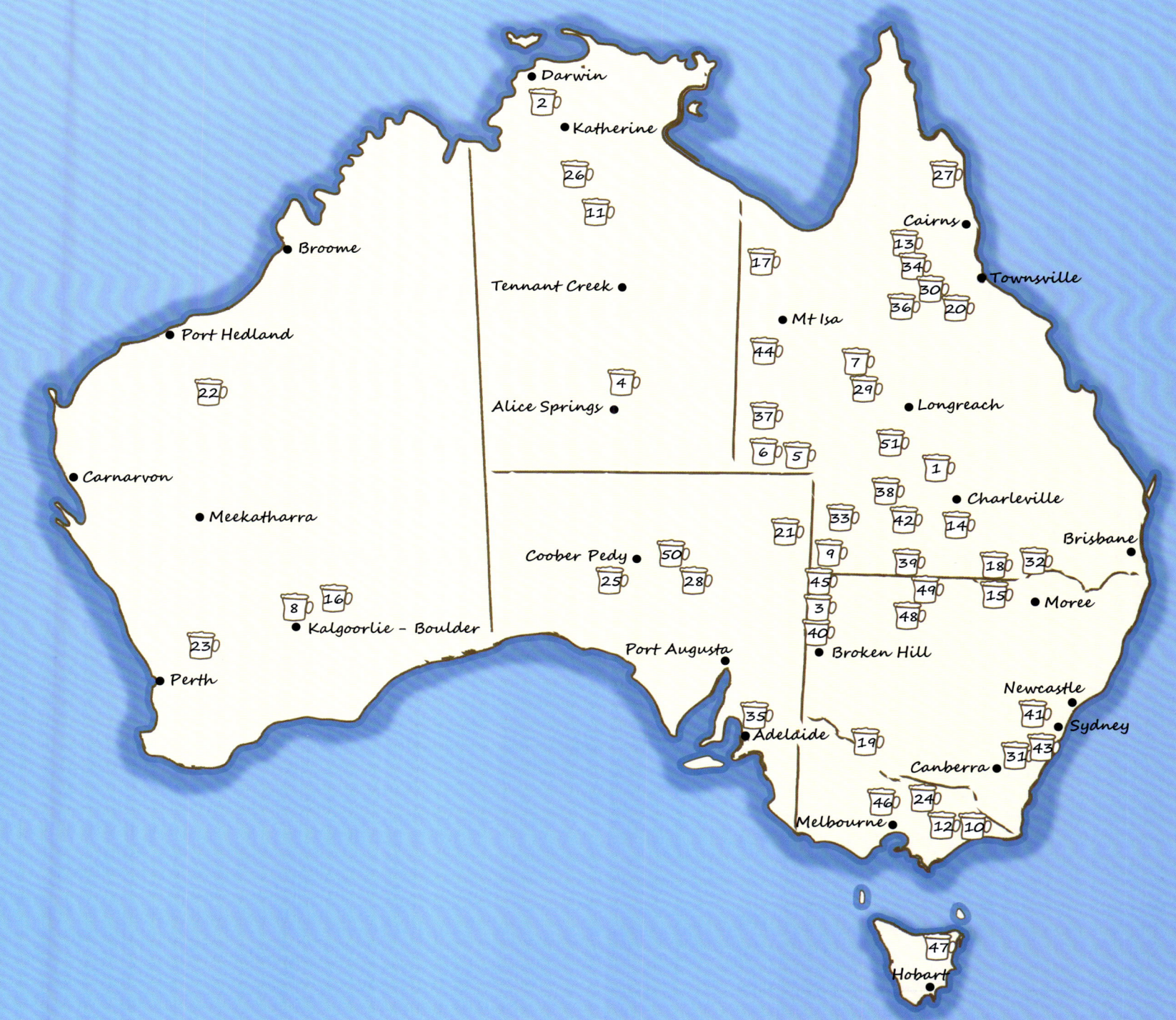

INTRODUCTION

Australia's bush pubs are an integral part of our social fabric; woven with colourful characters that helped shape our vast and remote areas, well away from the hustle and bustle of the cities. Like many of our well known landmarks, these humble establishments too are icons, many having stood the test of time when they once served almost frenetic metropolises that are today, in some cases, little more than ghost towns. In the enduring outback spirit, these venues are the cornerstones of the bush, dispensing their own unique brand of hospitality. A meeting place for locals and a welcome sight for travellers.

The pubs within these pages are a selection of both iconic and more obscure outback drinking spots, many of which have played an undisputed role in our folklore. The second edition of this book was needed when several pubs closed in the early 2010s. Since that 2016 edition, two lovely old pubs (the Ora Banda and Tattersalls) have sadly burnt down and two others have closed indefinitely. For this third edition we have replaced these with a handful of what we believe are very worthy choices. Covid was not kind to many bush pubs, so it's a joy to see that the great majority came through with their doors open. As you'll appreciate, this book is by no means a complete rundown of each and every bush pub to be found throughout Australia. Apart from being a monumental task in itself, it would be absolute punishment for our long suffering livers!

This book is partly a history book, partly travel guide and partly photographic journey to some of our best loved bush watering holes. You may agree or disagree with some of our choices, or even reckon we've missed out on a great bush pub. If this is the case please drop us a note (you'll find the address towards the back of the book) and we may well look at these in another edition.

Many of our featured pubs stem from the goldrush days when towns sprung into existence literally overnight. Some towns boasted almost an obscene number of pubs and illegal grog shanties relative to their populations. Take Queensland's Ravenswood, which at its peak was home to around 4500, but supported almost 40 pubs. Kookynie's Grand Hotel and Milparinka's Albert Hotel are other good examples of surviving gold town pubs. Other hotels were once part of the web-like stage coach network which criss-crossed much of eastern Australia. The best known of these firms was Cobb & Co who used these establishments to stable fresh horses and provide meals and accommodation for their travel weary passengers. Middleton Hotel and Hungerford's Royal Mail Hotel are relatively authentic reminders of these glory days of coach travel.

Some bush pubs are rather elaborate affairs, considering their locations. Take the impressive Marree Hotel, a handsome two storey sandstone structure which once served the bustling railway town on the edge of the desert. These days things are much quieter in Marree, and the hotel looks almost out of place, standing sentinel against a vast desert backdrop. Ravenswood's Imperial Hotel also fits this bill. Some pubs, such as the Larrimah, are simple buildings constructed of recycled material like steel pipe and corrugated iron, which reflects their locations as much as their purpose. However, all of the bush pubs featured have one thing in common: character.

But without doubt the unsung heroes of our bush pubs are the publicans who keep the tradition of bush hospitality alive and well. From us both, thank you to all the publicans whose pubs are featured in this book. You warmly welcomed us and without hesitation let us wander around your pubs, collecting information and taking photographs.

We would also like to thank several contributors who have helped us with researching the four new pubs included in this edition: Louise Denton, Simon Punch, Erin Jordan, Robbo and Katrina at Betoota, and several other obliging publicans.

Cheers,

The Bush Pubs

ADAVALE PUB

This remote outback Queensland settlement had once seen more prosperous times, but today's Adavale, with its pub and a few houses provides a stark reminder of the fragility of remote outback outposts.

Adavale Pub
Shepherd Street, Adavale
Queensland
0456 692555

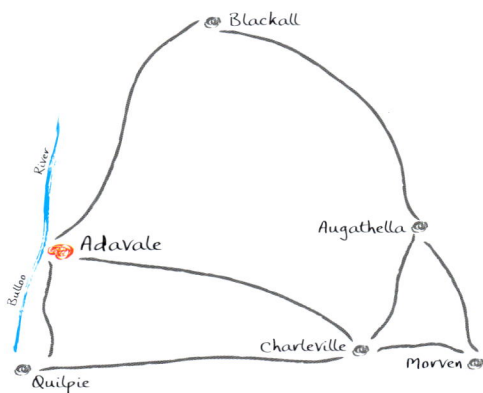

Gazetted as a town in 1880, the town's first hotel, the Imperial, swung open its doors for business the same year. Opal mining, along with the growth of the area's pastoral enterprises and the commencement of Cobb & Co coaches saw Adavale soon established as an important centre. The town grew to a population of around 2500 persons and boasted all the required amenities including government buildings, a shire office, butcher, baker and a cordial factory just to name a few.

But the coming of the railway to nearby Quilpie in 1917 heralded the beginning of the end of Adavale's prosperity. Many of the town's buildings, including the Great Western Hotel, were relocated to Quilpie.

In 1930 the Adavale Shire Council was dissolved and the region's administrative base moved to Quilpie. In 1963 torrential rains caused massive flooding of the Blackwater Creek, destroying many of the town's remaining buildings, almost sealing the fate of the struggling community.

The building in which the current Adavale Pub dispenses its hospitality was built in 1958 as the general store by Patrick Kennedy. Surviving the 1963 floods it was moved from Klugh Street to its present location in Shepherd Street. The timber framed, weatherboard clad structure boasts a small front bar and lounge area with a pool table, and an inviting front verandah.

Ada's veil

There are often quirky yarns relating to the plethora of unique Australian place names and Adavale is no exception. But who was Ada?

Well, according to Koss Siwers, publican of the Adavale Pub, local folklore suggests the town got its name from the new wife of a local landowner, Ernst Stevens. Stevens was the then member for Warrego and would later go on to become a member of the Queensland Legislative Council.

Allegedly, sometime in the very late 1870s Stevens was travelling to his Imbadulla and Injamulla runs, which had been leased by him since 1869. These runs were later consolidated to form Tintinchilla Station, which was then to become part of the vast Milo & Welford holdings. Fording the crossing of Blackwater Creek near where a fledgling settlement was to begin, a gust of wind dislodged Stevens' new bride's veil from her hat. The party was being accompanied by a stockman under the husband's employ who exclaimed 'There goes Mrs Ada's veil!' The stockman promptly dismounted his horse to retrieve the wayward veil, then raced over to the horse drawn buggy, retuning the headwear to his boss's wife.

Shortly after the name was bestowed upon the newly gazetted township, but with a change to the spelling, being named Adavale.

A less nostalgic story is that it is believed the town to have been named for the wife of the then Queensland Surveyor-General, William Alcock Tully. But interestingly, neither of his two wives were named Ada!

Maybe it's a tale cobbled together by the flickering light of a campfire and retold countless times in a grog fuelled bar, but a good yarn nonetheless.

ADELAIDE RIVER INN

Charles Todd's telegraph line caused a camp to be created at Adelaide River, which was later augmented by gold miners and those supplying them. Adelaide River became a key base for the allies in the Second World War.

**Adelaide River Inn & Resort
Dogherty Street, Adelaide River
Northern Territory
(08) 8976 7047**

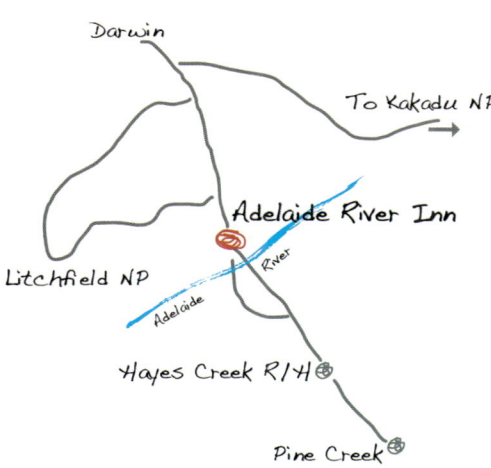

Established in 1870, Adelaide River was first a base for construction workers on the Overland Telegraph Line, before attracting miners when gold was discovered in 1872 at Pine Creek, 100 kilometres to the south.

Originally named the Q.C.E. Hotel, The Adelaide River Inn was built in 1874 on the southern side of the river, but quickly moved to the northern side where it remains today. Development of the area continued over the coming years: a railway line between Pine Creek and Darwin reached Adelaide River in 1888, nearby Mount Bundy station came to fruition in 1911 and construction on a road between Adelaide River and Darwin began in 1936.

The railway that serviced Adelaide River was closed in 1976, yet the infrastructure remains today as home to a museum as a part of the Adelaide River Railway Heritage Precinct. Original equipment from the 1880s is on display, along with wartime relics such as machine guns and ammunition. The Ghan, the cross-country railway service from Port Augusta in South Australia to Darwin was operational by 2004, and saw a third Adelaide River bridge constructed to service the railway.

The town still serves as an important rest stop for travellers, the Adelaide River Inn being a friendly, old-style country pub, comprising the Bar 303, Digger's Bistro and extensive, relaxed tropical gardens. Full of character and old charm, Bar 303 reflects its history in the name - the 303 rifle being the weapon of choice for the Australian Army in World War II.

Filled with memorabilia and photographs sharing the town's history, the pub is also home to Charlie, the buffalo famous for his role in the iconic movie Crocodile Dundee. A resident of Adelaide River, he passed away in 2000 and now stands proud on top of the bar. Jock the Croc is another thankfully inert resident of the pub, a 5-metre monster saltwater crocodile who was removed from Borroloola boat ramp due to attacking boats! The shady beer garden is a favourite stop-off for locals and travellers alike - a true Aussie experience.

The Second World War

Adelaide River played a significant role in the defense of Australia in World War II, accelerated by the Japanese Air Raids on Darwin in February 1942. The attacks caused people in Darwin to flee south and military activity in the region increased: several military airfields were built surrounding the town, and an artillery and weapons range at nearby Tortilla Flats. Adelaide River quickly become a tactical base for the area, with 30,000 US and Australian military personnel based here at the conflict's peak.

The surrounding outstations and facilities were bombed by the Japanese throughout 1942 and 1943, with the final attack on the town in November 1943. The Adelaide River War Cemetery was established in August 1942, one of the largest in Australia with over 430 service men and women and 63 civilians buried here. The cemetery was added to the Australian Commonwealth Heritage List in 2004.

Australian Bush Pubs | 21

ALBERT HOTEL

A gold rush to far western New South Wales in the late 1870s saw Milparinka proclaimed a town in 1880. The Albert Hotel is the last remaining hotel of four that once thrived in this outback post.

Albert Hotel
Loftus Street, Milparinka
New South Wales
(08) 8091 3863

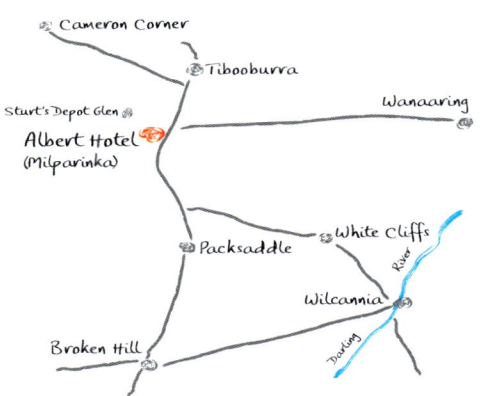

In March 1882 a publican's licence was granted to a Mr Patrick Kenny for a public house to serve the burgeoning goldfields of the state's far north-west. To be called 'The Albert', this, like many of the town's more substantial buildings, was constructed of local sandstone.

In 1890 the then owner of The Albert, Mr George Blore, built an additional stone building at the rear of the hotel to house race horses for the upcoming Christmas meet. Other publicans of note include Mr William Baker, who in June 1893 was charged for retailing from a licenced premises — he had sold a bag of sugar.

In 1897 Mr Thomas Hill became publican. It was during his time that the hotel came to the attention of local police. The Albert was marred by fighting, stealing and illegal selling of liquor.

Today, the front section of the Albert Hotel is what remains of the original structure, albeit in a renovated form. A walk through the front bar takes visitors into an internal courtyard with a fish pond — this area being surprisingly cool even during the warmer months. Located off this courtyard are a number of original guestrooms, with room six apparently haunted by the ghost of a young lady.

Regularly frequented by shearers, prospectors and travellers, there's certainly some interesting yarns to be had in the pub's front bar.

Milparinka Gold

When first proclaimed a town, there were also three other towns in the vicinity; Mt Browne, Albert and The Granites. Aside from Milparinka, only The Granites, later changing to its Aboriginal name of Tibooburra, remains.

Miners came to the region on foot, walking over 300 kilometres to the fields with pick, shovel and miner's right in hand. The lack of water was a major issue for miners, although mining continued in the area until the early 1920s. At this time public buildings such as the post office, school and courthouse closed — this was the beginning of the end of the town of Milparinka.

Captain Sturt's Expedition

Before the proclamation of Milparinka the area was visited by explorer Charles Sturt on his 1844 expedition to find the fabled inland sea.

Located to Milparinka's north-west, Depot Glen is a permanent waterhole where Sturt and his team were forced to camp for six months whilst waiting for rain to allow their retreat south to settled areas.

Sturt had his men build a rock cairn on the nearby hill, which he named after his second in command James Poole, who died during the expedition's enforced stay. He is buried to the east of Depot Glen.

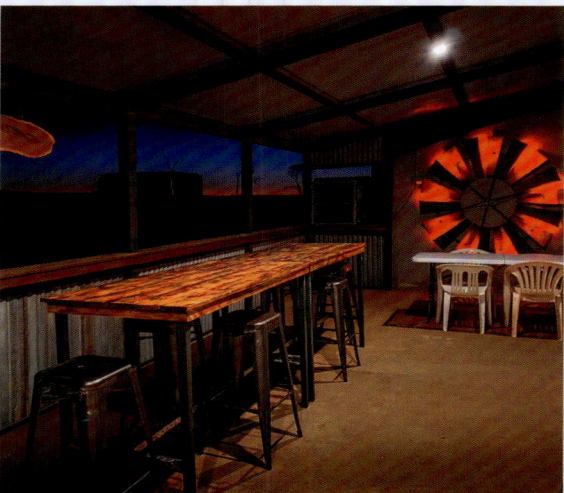

A tent township numbering almost 500 men grew beside a waterhole on Evelyn Creek as gold fever gripped the region.

BARROW CREEK HOTEL

Established in 1932, this unique bush pub stands beside the Stuart Highway, offering refreshments to the hordes of travellers who ply the road between Alice Springs and Tennant Creek.

**Barrow Creek Hotel
Stuart Hwy, Barrow Creek
Northern Territory
(08) 8956 9753**

Walking into the front bar of the Barrow Creek Hotel is like stumbling upon an oasis in the desert, especially if you're thirsty. Just about every nook and cranny in this place is plastered with some form of memorabilia (or pubobilia). There are road signs, hats, pictures, money in numerous denominations along with thousands of signatures adorning all available space. You could spend hours reading comments scrawled by travellers who have passed this way.

Built by the enterprising Kilgariff brothers out of hand-made concrete blocks, the hotel served its first drink on November 4th 1932 and before long was catering to the increasing number of travellers undertaking the adventurous journey along the old unsealed Stuart Highway.

Tom Roberts, affectionately known as the 'Mayor of Barrow Creek' worked at the telegraph station next door to the pub for almost 40 years, and was one of the hotel's colourful characters.

Station hands and droving teams where also regular visitors to the Barrow Creek Hotel. It was the ringers from these teams that initiated the tradition of pinning their last note with their name on it to the roof and walls of the hotel. This ensured that they had enough money to buy a drink on their next visit — a tradition that has continued to the current day with notes from around the world pinned to the walls of the hotel. Although it doesn't look like many people take their money down — it stays pinned to the walls as testament to their visit to Barrow Creek.

Into the Night

Images of the Barrow Creek Hotel were beamed around the world when the sleepy wayside inn bolted to prominence on Sunday July 15, 2001 after a road train pulled up out the front of the hotel in the early hours of the morning, the driver waking publican Les Pilton. Sitting terrified in the truck's cab was young Joanne Lees.

Joanne Lees recounted her experience of being attacked, bound and gagged by a solitary man who had stopped her and her partner, Peter Falconio along the Stuart Highway further north. It wasn't until later that day that the story hit the news headlines that Peter Falconio was missing.

Lees explained how Falconio had gone to the back of their van and spoke to the man. She then heard a loud bang and was attacked. Neither she or anyone else have ever seen Falconio again.

After an extensive man-hunt lasting 13 months, which stretched across the country, police apprehended a suspect in August 2002.

On December 13, 2005 Bradley John Murdoch was found guilty of the murder of Peter Falconio and was sentenced to life imprisonment with a 28 year non-parole period. To date Peter Falconio's body has never been found.

The pub at Barrow Creek is of architectural heritage value as being the first hotel built along the Stuart Highway.

BETOOTA HOTEL

Starting out life as a cattle station, then briefly a police station, the Betoota Hotel has seen good times and bad. However, it has seen a recent re-flowering thanks to the efforts of a determined fan.

Betoota Hotel
Birdsville Developmental Road, Birdsville
Queensland
0407 739798

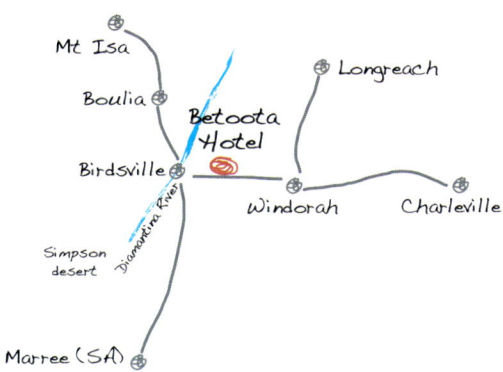

A custom station was built here back in 1885 with the purpose of monitoring and holding cattle being moved from state to state. In the early 1900s what had then become a cattle station was refashioned into a police station. However, once it was realised that there was little demand for a holding cell in the middle of the outback, this iconic building was transformed into the Betoota Hotel in 1922.

The Garrett family were the first owners of the hotel, followed by the Sanderson family. In 1953 Seigmund Remienko, a local grader driver commonly known as Ziggy, purchased the hotel and lived there by himself until he passed away in 1998. Apparently, Ziggy's dying wish was for the hotel to close and it slowly deteriorated.

In 2015, Robert Haken from Logan Victoria, who knew Ziggy in his youth, revisited the pub. He found the building vandalised and mistreated. Robert decided to bring this old country gem back to life, and taking matters into his own hands became the new owner of the Betoota Hotel in December 2017.

Due to its remote location and age, renovations were not easy. However in March 2020 the Betoota Hotel's doors opened to the public again. Unfortunately this was just at the same time as Covid restrictions affected the whole country; and the doors were once again closed. 'Robbo' took on the challenge and used the opportunity to do further renovations and additions to the pub.

During the renovations the hotel's original and much-loved façade and style was kept. Inside the doors, the hotel is a treasure trove of memorabilia, while outside the pub is surrounded by old vehicles and farm equipment. The revitalised Betoota Hotel has become a popular watering hole for travellers, and campers, in southwest Queensland.

BIRDSVILLE HOTEL

Lying at the northern end of the Birdsville Track, the Birdsville Hotel is without doubt Australia's most famous bush pub, and has become ingrained in outback folklore.

Birdsville Hotel
Adelaide Street, Birdsville
Queensland
(07) 4656 3244

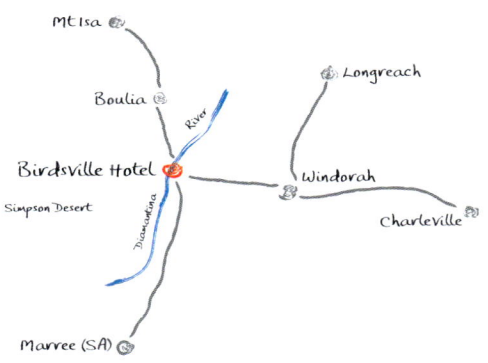

Birdsville is about as remote as a place gets, standing since 1884 on the edge of the vast Simpson Desert, Australia's last untamed frontier.

The hotel is forged into Australian folklore and travellers now make their pilgrimage to one of Australia's treasured icons, just as drovers, ringers and outback wanders have done for over a century. As they say, you haven't had a beer in the outback until you've had a beer at the Birdsville Pub!

These days the pub is a mecca for travellers, many who make the run up the once infamous Birdsville Track from Marree, about 500km to the south. Originally a stock route used by cattle drovers, the track is now a reasonably well-maintained road, but it still has the allure of the outback, as does this legendary pub.

Birdsville was first established as a stopover for drovers in the early 1880s. A customs post was erected soon after and before long the hotel came into existence. The original section of the hotel, which still stands, was built from whatever local rock could be found, including numerous small gibbers. These thick walls have some very uneven edges, but this just adds to the pub's appeal. The walls are whitewashed and often take on a gorgeous yellow glow as the late afternoon sun sinks into the Simpson Desert.

Inside, the pub is bursting with atmosphere. Dotted around the walls in the front bar are memorabilia and photographs, there's also the collection of hats above the bar.

Australian Bush Pubs

Green Lizard Room

Although most people head straight for the front bar of the famous pub, the hotel also boasts another bar. This is the oddly named Green Lizard Room.

According to a former publican, the Green Lizard Room was christened in honour of a cocktail made from Creme de Menthe.

Apparently late season rains had swept down from the Gulf Country, catching most towns in the Channel Country by surprise. Generally these remote outposts receive ample warning of impending wet weather, but this time the news came too late and literally overnight Birdsville and the surrounding districts were deluged with rain. The beer truck was due into town the following day!

The town was cut-off for nearly a month. Essential supplies being flown in by light plane, landing on a levelled sandhill. Within a week the pub was out of beer, then wine and rum until the only drink left were a few bottles of Creme de Menthe.

BLUE HEELER HOTEL

Named after Queensland's favourite working dog, the Blue Heeler Hotel was once one of three hotels in Kynuna. This delightful pub has been a favourite stop for thirsty travellers since 1889.

Blue Heeler Hotel
Matilda Hwy, Kynuna
Queensland
(07) 4746 8650

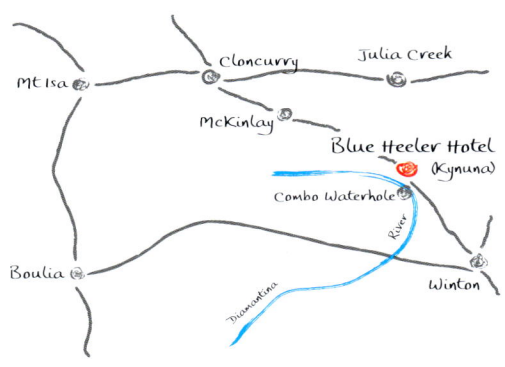

Originally known as Absolons Hotel, this timber weatherboard and corrugated iron hotel was built in 1889 and is still pretty much original. The large neon Blue Heeler on the roof was apparently a 99th birthday gift from the XXXX Brewery, and there's the large impressive fireplace that was built by the late RM Williams for the hotel's 100th birthday. Even with these newer additions the pub still retains much of its rustic charm.

This pub also played a role in one of Australia's best known songs. In 1894 Banjo Paterson visited the MacPherson family of nearby Dagworth Station. It was during a visit to the hotel that Robert MacPherson handed champagne through a pub window to the shearers outside. This gesture put to end the angry shearers strike of that year.

Paterson teamed this observation with the unrelated stories of the suicide of 'Frenchy' Hoffmeister and the drowning of another man in a billabong in the area.

Paterson then penned the words to a Scottish tune played on a zither by Miss MacPherson. The tune was 'Waltzing Matilda'. Paterson wrote of Waltzing Matilda shortly before his death; 'not a very great literary achievement, perhaps, but it has been sung in many parts of the world'.

The billabong in the song is believed to be the Combo Waterhole, which is located 20 kilometres east of The Blue Heeler Hotel.

Robert MacPherson abandoned Dagworth Station in 1930 due to drought and whilst at the then Absolons Hotel died from a heart attack.

BROAD ARROW TAVERN

The Broad Arrow Tavern is seen as something of a goldfield's icon. For over 100 years it has been providing beer, meals and a welcoming place for patrons to relax and unwind.

The Broad Arrow's new look

Broad Arrow Tavern
Railway Street, Broad Arrow
Western Australia
(08) 9024 2058

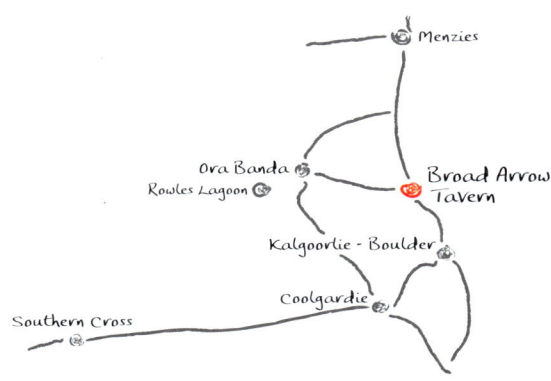

The corrugated iron clad Broad Arrow Tavern, or BAT as it is affectionately known, was established in 1896 and is the only surviving hotel, and indeed the only surviving business, from the town's heyday of 1900. Back then there were eight hotels, two breweries, two banks, a hospital, resident magistrate, stock exchange, and all the other associated businesses usually found in a town.

The town's two breweries, The Shamrock Brewery and the Broad Arrow Brewery were established in the late 1890s. Author Arthur Reid wrote in 1933 'that judging by the volume of beer brewed, Broad Arrow must have had the biggest beer drinking population in the world'.

Inside the BAT is a welcoming and very characterful front bar, a dining room off to the right and a pool room behind the bar. Every inch of the tavern's corrugated and weatherboard walls are signed by visitors, even the bar has signatures on its bright blue front. The dining room, however, has been saved from the permanent marker, its walls feature historic photos and articles of Broad Arrow and its surrounds.

In 1971 the hotel was featured in the movie, *The Nickel Queen*, the story of a female pub owner who stakes a mining claim on an area where nickel is found and who subsequently has an American company buy her out so she can live it up. The flick starred British actress Googie Withers and Australia's own 'Golden Tonsils' John Laws.

Nowadays Broad Arrow has a permanent population of six.

What's in a Name?

Apparently in 1893 a prospector by the name of O'Mara left Kalgoorlie telling his nephew he would leave a trail of broad arrows scratched on the ground, showing his direction of travel so that he could follow him later with a horse and cart.

Although Broad Arrow was the commonly used name, the town was originally gazetted as Kurawah in 1896, and then officially changed to Broad Arrow in 1897.

With good gold finds in 1898 leading to rapid settlement and major mining development, the area boomed. The richest mines in the early days were the Broad Arrow Consols, Hill End and the Golden Arrow. During the war years of 1914 to 1922, the major producers of gold were the Oversight and Tara leases. These two mines yielded 17 400 ounces of gold, a substantial quantity for the time.

The railway line from Kalgoorlie north to Menzies arrived in Broad Arrow in November 1897, just three months after its commencement. The line was completed to Menzies in March 1898. With water supply an ongoing problem for steam locomotives, five giant salt water condensers were built along the line to help alleviate the problem. The Broad Arrow Water Tower holds a 25 000 gallon cast iron water tank and is still used today by the town.

By the mid 1920s the rush to Broad Arrow was over and the town was then virtually abandoned.

CAMERON CORNER STORE

Although this remote watering hole, which sits on the Queensland side of the border fence, is 'modern' by bush pub standards, it has already forged a reputation as a classic since opening in 1989.

Cameron Corner Store
Cameron Corner via Tibooburra
Queensland
(08) 8091 3872

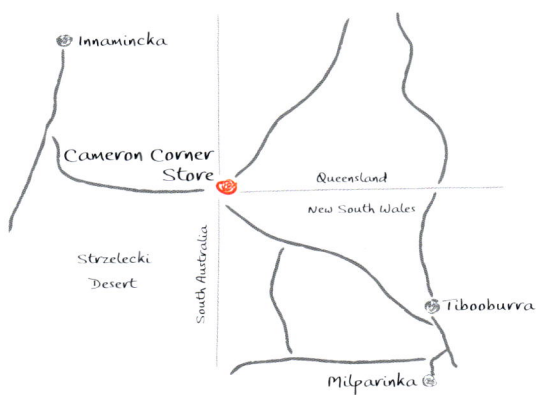

As far as outback bush pubs go, the Cameron Corner Store could easily be coined as the proverbial 'pub in the middle of nowhere!' It's 140 kilometres north-west from Tibooburra, its nearest neighbouring town of size. To add to the confusion, the 'Corner Store' is situated in Queensland, has a New South Wales postal address and rounds off with a South Australian telephone number!

Plonked right smack at the state border junctions of Queensland, New South Wales and South Australia, Cameron Corner is a popular destination for adventurous visitors exploring the corner country and is a popular stop for those travelling through from one state to the other.

It doesn't matter what time of the year you visit Cameron Corner Store, there's the likely chance that you'll meet workers from the oil and gas fields, shearers, truck drivers, doggers, gate keepers, farmers and shooters. There's generally someone about to have a yarn with. During the peak outback tourist season you are sure to come across a traveller or two stopping by for a drink or fuel and a chat about where they've been and where they're going. With such an eclectic group of customers you never know how your night at the Corner Store is going to pan out!

The Corner Store was built in 1989 by Sandy Nhall who spent two weeks at the Corner Post counting the number of visitors who stopped and then continued on. Sandy saw an opportunity and built the Corner Store. To date, there has only been two owners after Sandy.

The Surveyor's Saga

Cameron Corner bears the name of Scottish born surveyor John Cameron, who, along with Queensland surveyor George Watson, was employed by the NSW Lands Department to lead the first official survey party along the New South Wales-Queensland border between 1879 and 1881. This was along the 29th parallel south.

Starting the survey from the NSW town of Barringun after completing astronomical readings and building a 'zero' obelisk, Cameron and his party set out west towards the South Australian border on 2 September, 1879. Taking 12 months to complete the arduous task and hampered by searing heat, drought and flood, the party arrived (minus Watson who withdrew from the survey at the 100 mile post) at the intersection of the three states in September 1880. Cameron erected a wooden posted engraved 'Lat 29', along with the inscription 'Cameron'. The original wooden post, which is on display at the Tibooburra NPWS office, was replaced in June 1969 with a concrete pillar.

The party returned to Barringun and then started their survey to the east towards the MacIntyre River, finally completing the New South Wales-Queensland border survey in October 1881.

Of all the state border intersecting points on the Australian mainland, the most easily accessible is Cameron Corner — and it's got a pub!

COMMERCIAL HOTEL

The Commercial Hotel is a classic pub. Here, what you see is what you get and you'll find there is no pretence of it being anything other than a small town country hotel.

**Commercial Hotel
Dowling Street, Bendoc
Victoria
(02) 6458 1453**

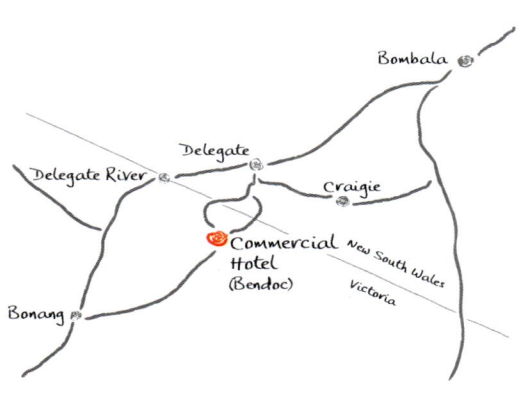

Bendoc is a small timber town located in Victoria's far East Gippsland, just south of the New South Wales border.

Bendoc's beginnings stem from an 1866 gold rush, and grew with the timber industry. West of town is the Delegate River Tunnel, a small tunnel hacked through solid rock by Chinese miners, and to the south of town are the verdant forests of the Errinundra Plateau.

The town's only drinking hole, the Commercial Hotel was first licenced in 1888, but originally stood opposite its current location. Half of the original building was burnt in a fire, and the remains of the other half are still standing opposite the hotel.

Not surprisingly, being in a timber town, the Commercial is built from local timber of rough sawn weatherboards, with internal architraves and door frames cut from wattle.

The Commercial saw new owners, Jono and Caroline take over in 2022, and they have been busy giving this wonderful old building some much needed, but very careful renovations. Jono commented, "we've had some good ideas as we've gone along and found some great historic things that can be put on display."

The new owners have rejuvenated the kitchen and are now serving meals to the passing trade, along with offering some basic accommodation.

Bendoc isn't on the well-worn tourist route, so you'll more than likely meet one of the few locals at the bar. Once you get this lot chatting there is no stopping them! If lucky, they may even let you in on where the monster trout which adorn the walls were caught.

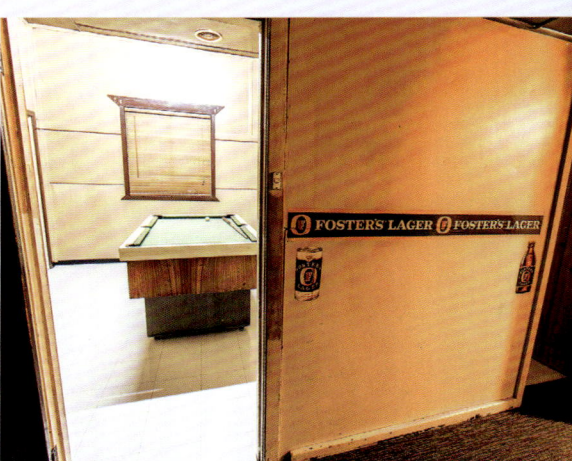

Australian Bush Pubs

DALY WATERS PUB

On any night this little outback pub can be packed to the rafters with travellers from all over the world, but it once was the haunt of drovers, flying mailmen and military personnel.

Daly Waters Pub
Main Street, Daly Waters
Northern Territory
(08) 8975 9927

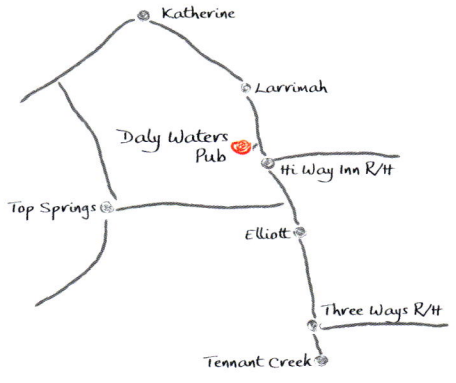

Famed Scottish explorer John McDouall Stuart named Daly Waters in 1862. Stuart was passing through the area on his third attempt to cross the Australian continent from south to north, and after having spent weeks cutting through almost impenetrable lancewood scrub he stumbled across a waterhole, where he and his party rested before continuing north.

Ten years later, in August 1872, the Overland Telegraph Line was completed and joined at Frews Ponds, south of Daly Waters. By 1887 a staff of five were located at the Telegraph Station.

In 1928 Bill and Henriette Pearce and their daughter Elizabeth settled at Daly Waters where they built a store to provide a service to travellers along the long, lonely stretch of road. The store then became the pub towards the end of the 1930s.

In 1930 an airfield was built to service the mail plane on its run between Daly Waters, Birdum and further destinations.

With the outbreak of World War II, the Daly Waters airfield was upgraded to become a base for both Australian and American bomber and fighter squadrons, flying bombing missions to PNG.

After the war Daly Waters' airfield was commissioned as Australia's first international airport, acting as a dispersal point for airmail to the United Kingdom as well as a re-fuelling strip for international passenger aircraft.

The Pearce's supplied meals for the airline staff

and to the growing number of passengers, and were renowned for their friendly service and unique bush hospitality.

When the war drew to a close, Daly Waters swiftly declined to a small community made up of aerodrome staff and local farmers. The Pearce's left the pub around this time, and in 1971 the aerodrome was officially closed.

Throughout all this the Daly Waters Pub managed to survive, and is still a popular watering hole for travellers from across Australia and from around the world.

Although Daly Waters is a 'tourist' pub, it still hasn't lost its character appeal, and unlike a lot of the Territory's hotels, which are basically roadhouses with a bar, Daly Waters is essentially a bush pub.

There's plenty of mementos from past visitors and memorabilia lining the walls.

During the dry season the pub offers up its nightly Beef & Barra dinner which is especially popular with the grey nomad set. Dished up in the outdoor barbecue area, travellers come far and wide to experience this unique Daly Waters phenomenon.

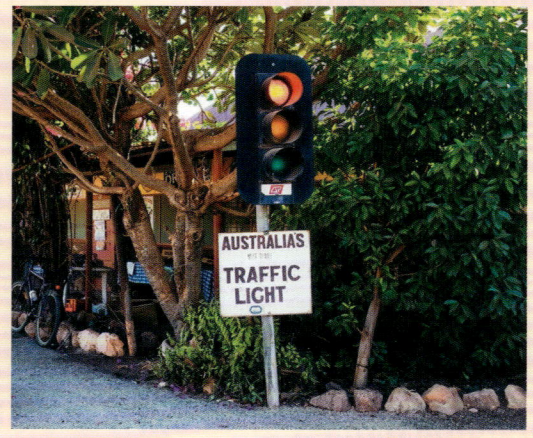

Many pub visitors have left their mark in the form of flags, currency, ID cards and anything else they might have been carrying on their journey.

DARGO HOTEL

High up in Victoria's alpine country, Dargo sits in a picturesque valley and has been a favoured stopping place for fortune-seeking goldminers, mountain cattlemen and travellers since the 1860s.

Dargo Hotel
Lind Avenue, Dargo
Victoria
(03) 5140 1231

Dargo grew into a major stopover point in the 1860s when miners would stop at the village for fresh supplies and a night at the pub before heading to the uncertainty of the goldfields. There were a number of drinking establishments operating in Dargo at that time and it is said that intoxicated prospectors would often stagger out of the hotels into Dargo's cold night air, only to be found the next morning with beards frozen solidly into the puddles in which they had fallen!

Patrick Coloe established a new hotel at Dargo in 1881. Centrally located opposite the courthouse, The Bridge Hotel supposedly soon became a popular venue and offered good accommodation. By 1896 The Bridge Hotel was the town's only remaining licenced hotel, but in March 1899 the hotel was destroyed by fire, and rebuilt from demolished buildings from the deserted gold township of Grant.

The Bridge Hotel was taken over by Dan Hurley in 1913 and the hotel remained within the Hurley family for almost 70 years. In the mid 1980s the hotel changed its name to the Dargo Hotel.

Apparently the old timers weren't too happy when electricity came to town, the newfangled way of serving the beer cold from a temprite, as opposed to cellar temperature, offered up a jar of ale far too cold for them!

A great example of a high country hotel, the timber and iron building is surrounded by a large verandah on two sides. Inside there is a front bar with a large dining room off to one side.

EINASLEIGH HOTEL

The Einasleigh Hotel was built in 1909. Originally known as the Central Hotel, it was one of the town's five hotels to be built and today survives as Einasleigh's sole watering hole.

Einasleigh Hotel
Daintree Street, Einasleigh
Queensland
(07) 4062 5222

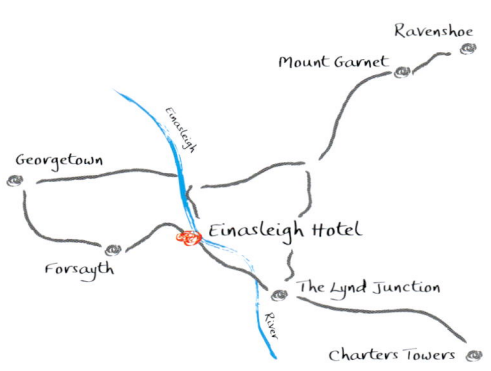

Nestled at the eastern edge of the Newcastle Range on the banks of the Copperfield River, the one-time copper mining town of Einasleigh is surrounded by unique savannahland scenery featuring flat top hills which seem to miraculously sprout out of the grasslands. Gazetted as a town in 1900 to service the copper mine at nearby Copperfield Gorge, the town ebbed and flowed with the boom and bust times of the mine.

For a brief period around 1910 when the rail line opened, Einasleigh became a prosperous township, serving as the supply centre for the Oaks gold rush. But by 1920 Einasleigh was almost a ghost town.

Originally known as The Central Hotel, the hotel and adjacent dance hall were built in 1909. By the end of 1910 The Central was one of five licensed hotels; however, by 1932 The Central was the town's sole remaining pub. The name changed to the Einasleigh in 1999.

Constructed in typical north Queensland style, the two storey timber framed, weatherboard building overlooks the town common and Einasleigh Gorge. It was placed on the state's heritage list in 2006.

Downstairs is the main bar - the bar's top is part of the dance floor from the old town hall. A room on the other side of the hallway is home to the publican's rather intriguing 'miniature' collection - a superb display of handmade depictions of everyday life. Ask at the bar to have a look.

Upstairs are ten guest rooms which, it is said, hosts the pub's resident ghost of a woman whose baby drowned in the river across the way.

Copperfield

The Einasleigh copper deposit was discovered in 1886 by Richard Daintree, the then Government's North Queensland Geologist, and was one of the earliest mineral discoveries in the Gulf Savannah. Known as The Lynd Mine, it was worked intermittently up until around 1898 when it became virtually abandoned. The mine reopened on a much larger scale in 1900. At the same time a town site was laid out, although a number of buildings, including a hotel, already existed at a shanty town what was then known as Copperfield.

In 1902 a small blast furnace was built for smelting ore, however transport costs to bring in smelting coke by camel trains saw the project marginal at best. The mine closed just a few years later but again reopened in 1906. By 1909 the New Einasleigh Copper Mine employed over 100 men.

When the Etheridge Railway to Forsayth opened in 1910, this allowed, for the first time, the economic cartage of ore to Chillagoe and by 1913 the Einasleigh Mine was the main supplier of copper ore to the Chillagoe Smelters.

Mining ceased in 1914 when the Chillagoe Smelters closed, but it operated again from 1920 to 1922 before closing due to dwindling ore reserves and the post-war drop in the world-wide copper price.

The Savannahlander train service runs weekly through Einasleigh and is renowned as one of the only Queensland trains that will actually stop outside a pub.

Australian Bush Pubs | 73

GLADSTONE HOTEL

Wyandra's second pub was built in 1889 and named the Gladstone. After burning to the ground in 1927, the hotel was rebuilt and is still pretty much the same today as when it reopened in 1929.

Gladstone Hotel
Railway Street, Wyandra
Queensland
(07) 4654 0273

The Gladstone Hotel is the only remaining hotel in Wyandra, and not much has changed at the single storey, timber and corrugated iron building.

The interior of the Gladstone Hotel is clean and sparse. There are no bras, undies, hats or t-shirts hanging from the ceiling; the walls are devoid of scribbles, business cards and overseas licences; there are no pin boards of photographs of partying backpackers — Wyandra is a little too far off the well-worn tourist route for this caper. It's a pleasant change for a bush pub.

Walking in off the street beneath the wide shady verandah you enter the main bar room. The bar — long by bush pub standards — wraps around in an L shape, and the hotel's original cellar is still below it. The separate dining room is off to the side with a warming wood heater. There is also a number of guest rooms for those staying the night.

Wyandra sits on the banks of the Warrego River, north of Cunnamulla and was a Cobb & Co stop on the Cunnamulla to Charleville run.

The railway from Charleville reached town in 1897 and in the following year it was extended to Cunnamulla. These were the heady days of Wyandra; with the railway came passenger, freight and mail transport, as well as a rail ambulance.

After the introduction of road freight the railway wasn't used as extensively as it once was and with its closure saw a decline in the town's prosperity.

About sixty people now live in Wyandra.

GLENGARRY HILTON

The sign says 'Welcome to the World Famous Glengarry Hilton'. We're not sure whose world it's famous in, but the Glengarry is nothing like any other Hilton you'll have visited!

**Glengarry Hilton
Glengarry Opal Fields
New South Wales
(02) 6829 3983**

Situated within the heart of the Glengarry Opal Fields, the Glengarry Hilton is a popular oasis with opal gougers who relax under the shady breezeway between the bar and main building. The pub's a huge ramshackle space set-off with a rustic collection of handmade timber furniture.

The bar resembles a corrugated iron garden shed, the likes you'd find in the average suburban backyard, while the main part of the pub houses a pool table, dining area and a couple of slow combustion wood heaters for those chilly midwinter opal field nights.

Surrounded by a parched landscape, it'll come as no suprise that at day's end you'll come across someone enjoying a couple of 'quite ones' at the Glengarry Hilton. There's a carved sign on the pub's door which reads: 'Trading Hours 6am to 6am 8 days a week CLOSED NEVER'.

This is a bush pub with stacks of character and there's a lot of human characters there too.

The Glengarry and neighbouring Grawin opal fields are an interesting destination to the west of Lightning Ridge and north-west of Walgett. The road into the Glengarry Hilton snakes its way past open mine shafts — the fields littered with mullock heaps and assorted mining machinery made from disused cars, trucks or any other types of mechanical item that could be utilised. Some of the residents live in small tin huts, while others boast more elaborate abodes, some even sporting well maintained flower gardens!

GRAND HOTEL

The real estate adage of 'Location, location, location' was the saving grace for the Grand Hotel at Kookynie. As the town's other six hotels ceased trading one by one, the Grand lived on!

Grand Hotel
Britannia Street, Kookynie
Western Australia
(08) 9031 3010

Trading since November 1902, the Grand Hotel was described at the time as not one of the 'grandest' hotels in town. Today, though, the Grand Hotel evokes a grandeur of its own in the once prosperous mining town. Internally it has fabulously high ceilings, large hallways, wide doorways and pressed metal ceilings with ceiling roses. On the walls of the main hallway hangs a collection of framed history, pictures and maps along with an assortment of rusty old tools from a bygone era.

Whilst patronage of the other six licenced hotels in the town slowly declined after the declaration of the Great War, the Grand Hotel managed to survive, most likely due to its location being directly opposite the railway station. This hotel, unlike the others, was the first and last stopping point in town for all those travelling by train, four of which arrived daily from Kalgoorlie.

In its heyday Kookynie was a town with 400 buildings and a resident population of around 3,500, with a similar number of transients. The town even boasted its own swimming baths and a booming red light district run by Japanese ladies.

Of the 400 buildings in Kookynie, there were seven licenced hotels and four private hotels. At the time private hotels were only permitted to serve alcohol to their house guests. However, house guests were also allowed to invite along seven of their own guests. Luckily, the town had its own brewery, so the pubs never ran dry.

The Beginning of the End

Kookynie was born from gold with the first leases taken up in 1895. In 1897 one of these leases was purchased by the London-owned Cosmopolitan Proprietary Ltd. The Cosmopolitan was to extract the largest amount of gold from the area, however its demise came in 1910 when the company halted operations due to constant flooding of the mine. Generally not an issue for most gold mining regions, on the Kookynie leases underground artesian reservoirs proved problematic. The underground waters were pumped to the surface and then channelled away. Sometimes the excess waters overflowed, ending up in the town's streets causing minor flooding. The cost to constantly run the pumps day and night eventually made the mine unviable and the Cosmopolitan Mine ceased operations.

The ruins of two of the town's other hotels, The Cosmopolitan and The National are only a short stroll from the Grand. The National was said to have been 'elegant with comfort', which compared most favourably to 'similar establishments in the larger centres of population'.

At the end of World War I, as the town's population dwindled most of the buildings were dismantled, with materials recycled or buildings relocated to other areas.

All of Kookynie's seven hotels, bar the Grand Hotel, ceased to trade around 1911 when the ore ran out and the mines closed.

GREGORY DOWNS HOTEL

A gulf country classic since its beginnings in the late 1800s, the Gregory Downs Hotel still dispenses hospitality to all who venture through the region.

Gregory Downs Hotel
Wills Developmental Road, Gregory
Queensland
(07) 4748 5566

Gregory Downs was first settled by the Watson brothers in 1877. The trio left Walwa, on the Murray River, the previous year to overland to the Gulf, with a plan to purchase livestock en route. They made a selection on the banks of the Gregory River as a base for their enterprise where they built a one roomed log hut — the site of the present day Gregory Downs Hotel.

With the success of their general store in Burketown which they had set up a fews years previous, the Watsons then started a pub and store at the site of their homestead at Gregory Downs to service the coach passengers on the Camooweal to Burketown route. With the passing of time travellers started to became a nuisance in the operation of their pastoral operations so the homestead was relocated across the Gregory River, leaving the now well patronised store and pub in place.

The business changed hands a number of times in the intervening years, with one of the more popular publicans being Emily Barrett — known as 'Auntie' Barrett to all — who was renown far and wide for her wonderful cooking. The hotel soon became a home away from home for stockmen on the surrounding properties. 'Auntie' Barrett held the license until her death in 1933.

The timber framed, weatherboard clad building consists of a large public bar and dining area. A shady verandah covers the front and one side and makes a top spot to relax.

Gregory is a popular stopover for travellers venturing to Lawn Hill National Park.

HEBEL HOTEL

There's been a hotel at the border crossing settlement of Hebel since 1894. More than 100 years on the pub still offers up to travellers, stockmen and shearers a cleansing ale or two in the hotel's bar.

Hebel Hotel
William Street, Hebel
Queensland
(07) 4625 0923

One of the great things about the Hebel Hotel is that it looks like it's always been there, sitting quietly beside the road serving passing travellers as it has done for well over a century. It's built in typical western Queensland style; weatherboard clad walls with a corrugated iron roof and a shady verandah out front.

In 1894 the Hebel Hotel officially opened as a Cobb & Co changing station, later commencing operations as a hotel. Still standing outside the pub are a number of rickety old posts which are the original horse hitching rails.

Inside, the pub consists of a front bar, with both the walls and ceiling clad with lining boards. There's a collection of shearing memorabilia with hand shears, wool bale bags, bale hooks, combs and station brands on the walls. Shearers still stop by the hotel for a couple of 'brown lemonades' after cut-out. The front verandah is a popular spot for the locals, especially in the late afternoons and on those warm western downs evenings, to sit and spin a few yarns.

The 'blink and you'll miss it' settlement of Hebel is located just north of the New South Wales/Queensland border on the Castlereagh Highway, about midway between the towns of Walgett in New South Wales and St George in Queensland.

Established in 1889 as a customs post, the burgeoning settlement was originally given the name Kelly's Point, allegedly after bushranger Dan Kelly, who is said to have resided in the area for a time, but this story seems rather highly unlikely.

Australian Bush Pubs

Australian Bush Pubs

Apparently the town's name was changed to Hebel in the early 1890s after a German family that lived in town.

Back in the days before 'Tidy Town Awards' were in vogue, Hebel had the dubious distinction of hosting one of the largest bottle dumps in the country. Popular folklore has it that from the mid 1940s up until it was bulldozed in the mid 1960s, the collection of empty beer and rum bottles beside the pub measured 36 feet long by 21 feet wide. This enormous pile of glass could be seen from 30 000 feet above by planes en route from Sydney to Hong Kong — they used it as a navigation aid!

Along with bushrangers, and others of a less sinister nature, Lightning Ridge based artist John Murray has also left his mark on the Hebel Hotel with his quirky paintings. His work has enhanced the look and feel of this great little pub, giving it a uniqueness.

You'll find John's photo-realistic art is scattered throughout the hotel, on the exterior walls and doors, those fake front windows and obviously on the tin roof. And those whimsical animals, well, they have their own individual personalities and charm — just like the drinkers breasting the bar at the hotel.

The Hebel Hotel is one of those bush pubs you simply can't drive past without wanting to call in, no matter what time of day!

HOMEBUSH HOTEL

The route between Balranald and Ivanhoe was once dotted with roadside inns, but today the Homebush Hotel is the only surviving watering hole for travellers along this long, lonely stretch of road.

Homebush Hotel
Ivanhoe Road, Penarie
New South Wales
(03) 5020 6803

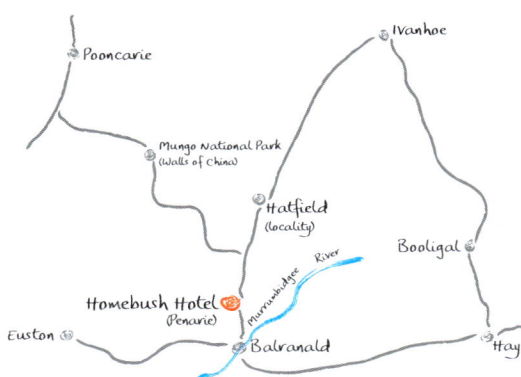

G'day. Welcome to the Homebush' was the greeting as we walked through the front door of the picturesque little pub at Penarie, about 27 kilometres north of Balranald on the road to Ivanhoe. The hotel stands sentinel over a vast, open plain, with little else surrounding it besides a few trees here and there to break the mirage. We instantly liked the place.

The external facade of the hotel hides a front bar, together with a dining area and pool table which is housed inside a large room with a centrally located fireplace. But the front bar is the pub's focal point.

The Homebush Hotel is well patronised with people from all walks of life stopping by for a coldie. On any given day you'll come across shearers, farmers, truck drivers, timber cutters, travellers and even charcoal burners holding court at the bar. The pub's also becoming an increasingly popular stopover for visitors to and from the nearby World Heritage Listed Mungo National Park.

In September 1860 the Burke and Wills expedition passed to the west of where the hotel now stands on their way to Menindee after crossing the Murrumbidgee River at Balranald. They noted that there was already significant settlement occuring in the area.

Homebush Hotel commenced business in 1878 and has been dishing out its unique brand of outback hospitality ever since. Hanging on one of the inside walls is an honour board listing the hotel's numerous publicans, commencing with Michael Dowdican, the Homebush's foundation inn keeper. Dowdican originally owned the land on which the pub was built, located at the junction of the Balranald, Ivanhoe and Oxley roads. Dowdican's stay at the hotel lasted until 1896 when William Wilkinson became licensee.

During these early years of settlement, pastoralists began pushing further west from the Riverina in search of grazing country. As the region become more settled, the route between Balranald and Ivanhoe was transformed into a well-worn track, being regularly used to transport sizable wool clips by horse-drawn wagon to ports along the Murray River. It was also trafficked by prospectors heading to the western goldfields, who no doubt saw the little settlement of Penarie with its pub as a place to rest up before venturing further into the unknown.

Roadside inns and hotels were built to serve the passing trade. A popular custom at the time was to plant a pepper tree out the front of these lonely roadside establishments. These days, a lone pepper tree silhouetted against the backdrop of a simmering saltbush plain represents the one time existence of a long gone hotel.

Michael Dowdican purchased land at the Balranald-Ivanhoe-Oxley road junction and built the Homebush Hotel.

Australian Bush Pubs | 101

IMPERIAL HOTEL

The first Imperial Hotel was built by Jim Delaney and burnt to the ground less than a year later. The present hotel was built in 1902 — this time from brick, not wood.

Imperial Hotel
Macrossan Street, Ravenswood
Queensland
(07) 4770 2131

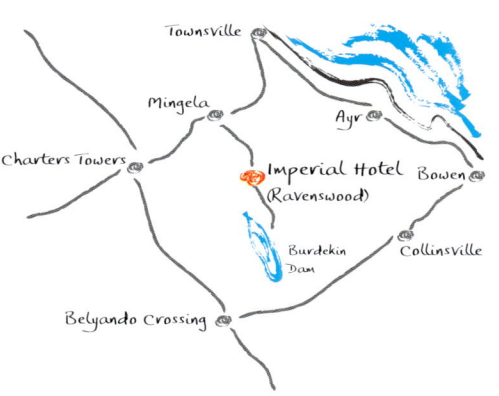

With the discovery of gold in 1868 and the subsequent development of mining operations through to the early 1900s, the township of Ravenswood grew to around 4500 residents and at its peak boasted more than 30 hotels. Several historic buildings remain from this period, including a couple of shops and the impressively ornate Imperial Hotel.

However, the town's heady days were to be short lived. The tumultuous industrial strike of 1912 and the start of the Great War in 1914 saw the decline of mining. By 1917 mining had ceased and the town was virtually deserted.

Today, two hotels remain, the Railway and the Imperial. Both are impressive buildings from a more prosperous time.

The first Imperial Hotel was built in 1901 by James Delaney during the height of the gold rush in Ravenswood. Six months later the timber structure burned to the ground. Unperturbed, in 1902 Delaney re-built the hotel from brick and timber, the one which remains today. The hotel remained within the Delaney family until the 1990s.

Essentially in its original state since it first opened well over a century ago, the Imperial is arguably one of the most intact examples of a hotel from that period. The impressive facade, complete with arched pediment and spires, commands its street scape presence while the bar, whose original fittings include a highly decorated timber and lead light dividing screen, makes this one of the finest historic hotel interiors in the country.

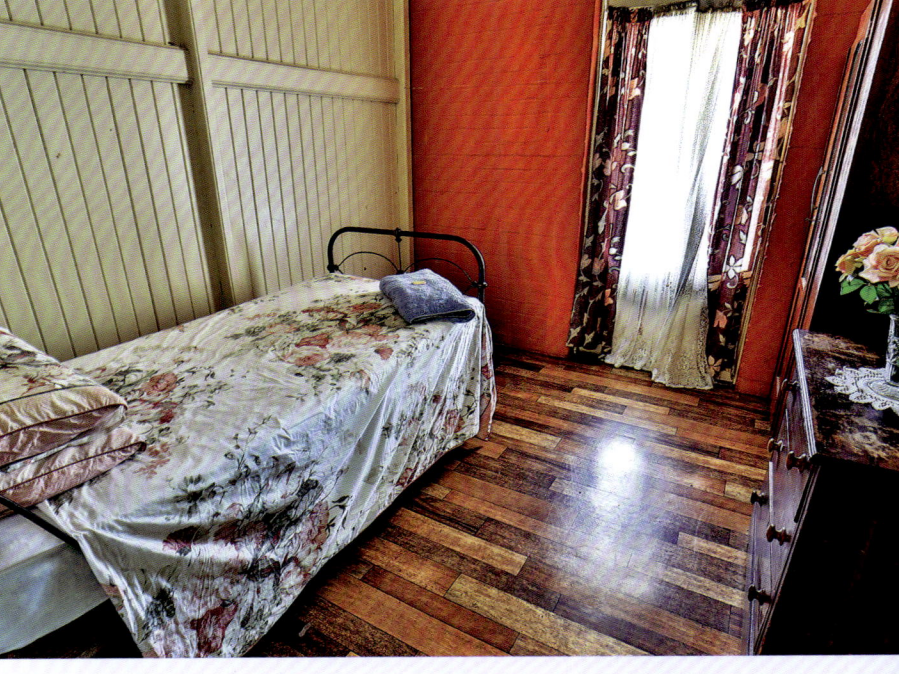

Australian Bush Pubs | **105**

INNAMINCKA HOTEL

In 1886, only 25 years after explorers Burke and Wills perished on the banks of Cooper Creek for the want of sustenance, the first hotel at the settlement of Innamincka was established.

Innamincka Hotel
South Terrace, Innamincka
South Australia
(08) 8675 9901

When the first hotel was set up on the banks of Cooper Creek in 1886, Innamincka was little more than a dusty outpost serving the hardy cattlemen who had started droving stock overland to the edge of the desert. The first European settlers were customs officers collecting taxes from droving parties crossing the border from Queensland.

The tiny settlement's pub operated in various guises until 1952 when the town itself virtually died. The pub then closed.

In the early 1970s the area experienced a surge in tourism and in 1973 a store was established. The hotel reopened with an accompanying motel which was re-named Cooper's Creek Hotel-Motel. In 1983, after the licence was suspended for a period, the hotel was again reopened and the name changed to Innamincka Hotel. This remote watering hole has seen many changes and renovations over the years and today's Innamincka Hotel is quite modern for an outback pub. Although the main bar area has changed little over the last lot of years, there is now a large dining room to cater for the seasonal influx of visitors — Sunday night dinners have always been a popular attraction.

Innamincka's remote location and connections with the Burke and Wills saga have made it a 'must visit' area on many people's travel itinerary. During the peak winter season the bar is likely to be frequented by travellers from all over Australia, plonked on one of the stools enjoying a drink.

And, after all our visits over the years, it's still a great spot to have a beer or two.

Burke, Wills & King at Cooper Creek

A party of seven men from the Victorian Exploring Expedition arrived on the banks of Cooper Creek on November 20 1860, on their quest to be the first men to traverse the Australian continent from south to north.

After establishing a depot at Bulla Bulla Waterhole to the north of present day Innamincka, Burke, Wills, King and Gray set off in the oppressive summer heat, instructing the party left behind at Cooper Creek depot to return to Melbourne if they did not return within three months. They were to be presumed perished or having taken an alternative return route.

After four months and five days Burke, Wills and King returned to Cooper Creek on 21 April, 1861 to find that the depot was deserted — the depot party had departed only hours prior. A blazed tree with the same date advised of buried supplies.

After a continuation of mishaps, both Burke and Wills died some months later of starvation on the banks of the Cooper. John King was cared for by a group of Aborigines until his rescue by Alfred Howitt in September that year. He was the party's sole survivor.

Located east of the hotel is Burke's grave site and the Dig Tree while to the west is the grave site of Wills and King's marker.

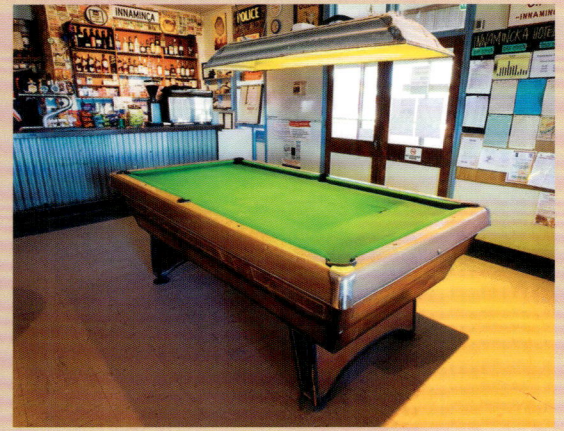

Innamincka is remote, its nearest town being Tibooburra, some 340 odd kilometres to the south-east via Warri Warri Gate.

IRONCLAD HOTEL

Marble Bar is listed in the Guinness Book of Records as being the hottest town in Australia. During late 1923 and early 1924, the town notched up 161 consecutive days over 38 degrees Celsius!

Ironclad Hotel
Francis Street, Marble Bar
Western Australia
(08) 9176 1066

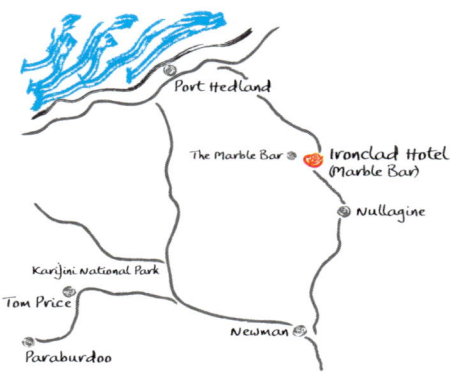

There is conjecture as to the origin of the name of Marble Bar's only remaining hotel, the Ironclad. Some sources suggest it was named after the richest mining claim in the area at the time, the Ironclad Lease, while others suggest a type of American boat — which operated on the Mississippi River at the time — provided inspiration, or was it simply named after the actual construction materials? It doesn't really matter either way, the Ironclad Hotel is just that, clad in iron. Even the pub's rustic interior has been given the corrugated and ripple iron treatment.

The Ironclad Hotel was built in 1892 at a time when there was an influx of prospectors to the East Pilbara goldfields. Originally, the Ironclad Hotel was one of two hotels in town; The Marble Bar Hotel which was opposite the Ironclad Hotel was de-licenced in 1915.

Except for a few renovations and additions over the years, the actual structure of the Ironclad Hotel hasn't changed much since it was first built. There are two bars, a back room with a pool table and a beer garden out the back with a small stage.

On the Coongan River, just five kilometres west of town is the colourful jasper stone bar which gold prospector Nathaniel Cook came across in the early 1880s. Cook, also a grazier, was looking for pasture for his drought affected sheep. Thinking the impressive jasper outcrop was marble, he named the area Marble Bar.

In 1888 alluvial gold was discovered on the Coongan River, beginning a rush to the area.

JENNACUBBINE TAVERN

Located in the Western Australian Wheatbelt, the Jennacubbine Tavern, or 'The Jenna' as it's locally known, has been serving locals and travellers for over 100 years, and is still one of the best spots to grab a steak in WA.

Jennacubbine Tavern
Collins Street, Jennacubbine
Western Australia
(08) 9623 2273

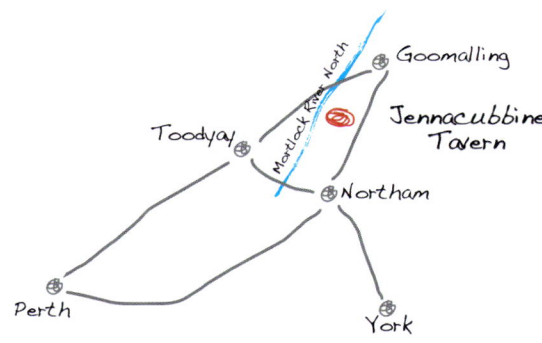

At first glance, The Jennacubbine Tavern looks like an oasis in an empty town, with its lush green beer garden and wide shady verandah. You could be forgiven for thinking the town itself, set amongst the wide-open spaces of West Australia's wheatbelt is deserted - that is until 4:00pm comes around, and the tavern opens its doors.

Established as a town in 1902, alongside the railway (as a siding between Northam and Goomalling) it initially consisted of the tavern, a general store, a couple of shops and eight houses on the main street, leading conveniently to the pub. The Tavern itself, back then the Jennacubbine Hotel, was constructed in 1898 for those travelling in the area. In 1902 it received its liquor licence under its first publican Archie Sydney Webb.

Jennacubbine was always a small settlement, but by the 1960s all that remained was the Tavern, the general store and one house. Then in 1970 the century-old general store burnt to the ground. A fire truck from Goomalling did attend, only to discover its onboard water tanks were dry from a previous fire; the town had no water hydrants and so the general store was sadly lost.

Despite the lack of people living in the town, The Jenna has continued to do a roaring trade with surrounding farmers, locals, and travellers alike. It's easy to see the allure of the pub. As soon as you enter the front door, you are greeted warmly by the bar staff and locals. The beer is cold, the footy or cricket is on and the delicious smell of steaks wafts through the air. Current owners Michelle and Brett put the pub's success down to the friendly locals, their renowned steaks and the beer garden (the largest in the wheatbelt).

The hanging portrait is of Captain Hugo Throssel. He was the officer in charge of the Jennacubbine Mounted Rifles and the first West Aussie (and only Light Horsemen) to be awarded a Victoria Cross in World War One.

KEVINGTON HOTEL

The Kevington Hotel, or the 'Kevi' as it is affectionately known, is the last remaining hotel in this part of Victoria from the heady gold rush days of the 1800s.

Kevington Hotel
Mansfield - Woods Point Road, Kevington
Victoria
0437 367740

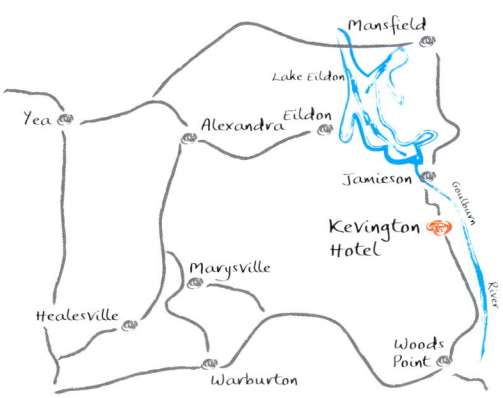

Established in 1862 as Garrett's Beerhouse at what was then called Macs Creek on the route between the goldfields of Jamieson and Gaffney's Creek, this quaint public house still retains a charm from a bygone era. Sitting under the pub's front verandah with a cleansing ale, it's not hard to imagine an endless string of prospectors, who after plying the track between the region's major goldfields, coming across this secluded watering hole and stopping in to quench their thirst.

As gold fever gripped the area the number of miners increased, as did the beerhouse's trade. With the passage of time the Garretts were able to construct a more substantial building on the site which was to became known as the Kevington Hotel, offering accommodation and meals for travellers.

The hotel remained in the Garrett family for another 95 years until they sold up in 1957.

The hotel is constructed of weatherboards with a corrugated iron roof. Walking in off the road you enter the front bar, while off to the side is a lounge area complete with a roaring log fire for those chilly winter days and nights. Follow the hallway and you come to a dining room, while there are a number of guest rooms a littler further out the back. The rear of the hotel sports a delightful, shady beer garden with the meandering Goulburn River passing by.

These days the area is a popular camping, fishing and 4WD touring destination and the pub's bar still dispenses refreshments to both locals and travellers as it has done for the past 150 or so years.

The Kevington has limited opening hours, so please call ahead if you plan on dropping by.

KINGOONYA HOTEL

Kingoonya Hotel is one of those great outback institutions with a varied past. It has had its fair share of trials and tribulations and is now once again dispensing good old-fashioned hospitality in the bush.

**Kingoonya Hotel
Kingoonya Terrace, Kingoonya
South Australia
(08) 8672 1002**

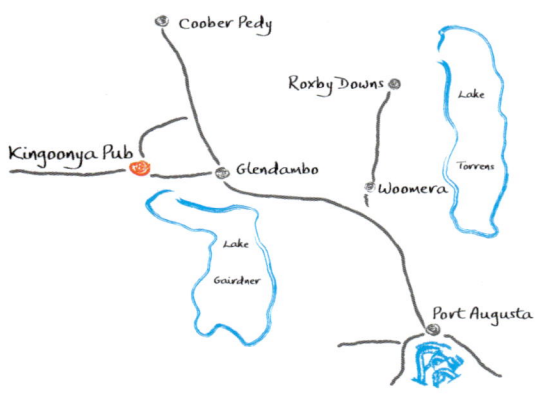

First opened in 1937 in what was then a thriving outback South Australian town, the Kingoonya Pub's prosperity was buoyed by passing trade along the Stuart Highway, the Trans-Continental Railway and helped by local graziers and shearers.

Interestingly, there were two applications to build and licence the town's first hotel. The 'favourite' with locals was Eileen Brett from Port Augusta, who was given the go-ahead after a hearing was held in the bar of the town's racecourse. The hotel was built in a record six months!

Eileen Brett, later Crosby, ran the hotel along with her husband until her death in 1960. The lease was then transferred to Eileen's son Neill, who, along with his wife, stayed on at the pub until 1971.

Then, in the early 1980s when the Stuart Highway was re-routed to the east, the death knell sounded for Kingoonya after many of the townfolk had their houses transported to the new Glendambo Village. In 1982 when the hotel's licence expired it was transferred to the new hotel/roadhouse at Glendambo. The pub closed. Kingoonya became a ghost town.

The hotel fell into a state of disrepair and was ravaged by vandals until an Adelaide man, Paul Dryga, who was passing through town, reasoned the hotel building would make an ideal base from which to operate his long-term mineral drilling explorations in the area. Settlement covenants precluded Dryga from reopening the old Kingoonya Hotel as a licenced pub. In 1997, ten years after his purchase of the building,

Australian Bush Pubs | 125

Dryga applied for and was granted a licence, after he reasoned that reopening the old pub at Kingoonya would pose no threat to the now well-establish Glendambo Hotel. In December 2003 the hotel recommenced business with a leasee, some 21 years after the call of 'last drinks'.

Dryga sold the pub in September 2005 to the Taylor family. They had long been passionate advocates of the hotel's history and remote outback location. After remaining closed for essential renovations, the pub reopened its doors in late 2006 and is again dispensing hospitality to travellers.

The pub still retains much of its charm. It's a substantial building constructed of concrete with a corrugated iron roof. There's a wide verandah around the front of the building — an ideal spot to relax in the late afternoon as the sun sinks in the western sky. Trainspotters are kept happy with the Trans-Continental Railway running past the front of the pub.

Inside, the original bar room has been reinstated, while the side verandah, which has been enclosed now serves as a casual dining area. A number of motel style guest rooms attached to the side of the pub complete the picture.

These days Kingoonya has a permanent population of less than ten people, so there's a good chance you'll meet one or two in the bar.

Kingoonya is reputed to have the widest main street in Australia, with cricket matches having been played on it!

LARRIMAH HOTEL

At 181.04 metres above sea level to the top of the bar, The Larrimah Hotel boasts the 'highest' bar in the Northern Territory. That's just one of the quirky things about this unique Top End bush pub.

**Larrimah Hotel
Mahony Street, Larrimah
Northern Territory
(08) 8975 9931**

In the local Aboriginal Yangman language, Larrimah means 'meeting place', an apt word for this friendly little Top End hotel. Enveloped by shady trees and a huge verandah, it makes an ideal place to get together. Originally frequented by railway workers, truckies and drovers, the pub is now a firm favourite with tourists travelling along the Stuart Highway.

The Larrimah Hotel was partly constructed of materials recycled from the dismantled Birdum Hotel, which was located seven kilometres south of Larrimah. The building itself is a 'Sidney Williams' construction — a bolted steel frame construction clad in corrugated iron with wide eaves. This style of prefabricated building was popular during the war years as it enabled the building to be erected quickly and also easily dismantled so it could be moved to another location if required.

When the North Australia Railway was extended to Birdum, Catherine and Tim O'Shea, who had previously built hotels in remote parts of the Northern Territory, seized the opportunity to build a hotel at the new railhead. The pub, which was opened in 1929, soon became a well established drinking hole for drovers, train crews and passengers travelling the railway between Darwin and Birdum.

Birdum's days as a town were short-lived. The area's black soil caused the north-south road to become impassable during the wet season while the military — it was now wartime — saw that the bridge along this road was a possible target for enemy attack. These factors resulted in the railhead being moved

north to the present day site of Larrimah in 1941.

Larrimah soon became a military town. When Darwin was bombed in February 1942 by the Japanese, coastal shipping became a precarious proposition, necessitating the need for overland road and rail transport. Convoys of trucks from Alice Springs and Mt Isa streamed in and out of Larrimah, their cargoes transferred to rail for the final leg to Darwin.

By late 1945 Birdum was abandoned. The hotel was dismantled and moved, becoming the Larrimah Hotel, which opened in 1952.

Former publican Sidney Smith, a man well-versed in the ways of gaining media publicity, thought that a large pink panther — with fishing rod, sitting beside a puddle out the front of the pub — would make a good story. Smith proposed that Larrimah had the Northern Territory's smallest freshwater lake, and although it looked shallow it was in fact so deep that a road-train disappeared into it!

In 2003 the pub's future looked grim when an order to condemn the rambling old building was served. The foresight of a dedicated bunch of people saw the hotel saved from demolition. And it's still offering that renowned Top End hospitality today.

The pub is immediately recognisable from the highway thanks to the large NT stubby and pink panther sitting outside.

LIONS DEN HOTEL

A north Queensland 'classic', the Lions Den Hotel is located south of Cooktown on the banks of the Little Annan River. Shaded by huge mango trees, the pub harks back to the days of old.

Lions Den Hotel
Shiptons Flat Road, Helenvale
Queensland
(07) 4060 3911

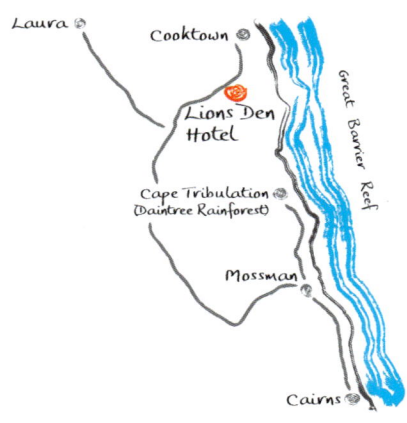

Built in 1875 out of bush poles and sawn timber and clad with corrugated iron inside and out, the Lions Den Hotel is set on the edge of lush north Queensland tropical rainforest. To the south is the famed World Heritage Listed Daintree Rainforest.

Popular legend has it that the pub took its name from a local tin mine, the Lions Den. Apparently the mine was nameless when a sailor by the name of Daniel, who had deserted his ship in Cooktown, showed up at the mine looking for work. The rookie employee, never having had to work underground before, was nicknamed 'Daniel in the Lions Den' by the mine's owner. From this came the mine's name as well as lending the moniker to the pub.

During the northern dry season, the Lions Den gets busy with travellers, especially with four-wheel drivers travelling the Bloomfield Track from Cape Tribulation north to Cooktown. It's also well patronised by the handful of locals and from the communities along the Bloomfield Track.

Outside there's a wide verandah fronting the pub, essential for those balmy tropical afternoons. Inside is a small front bar area along with a larger lounge bar cum dining area. The walls are plastered with countless names and signatures, along with a collection of anything and everything ranging from number plates, old bottles, hats, T-shirts and stubby holders. At the rear of the pub is a museum with a wonderful collection of old farm memorabilia and a natural history display of local snakes, fish, spiders and frogs.

Australian Bush Pubs | 135

MARREE HOTEL

Marree was once an important railway town as well as a base for the famous Afghan camel drivers who carried supplies to the outlying centres such as Oodnadatta, Birdsville and Alice Springs.

Marree Hotel
Railway Terrace, Marree
South Australia
(08) 8675 8344

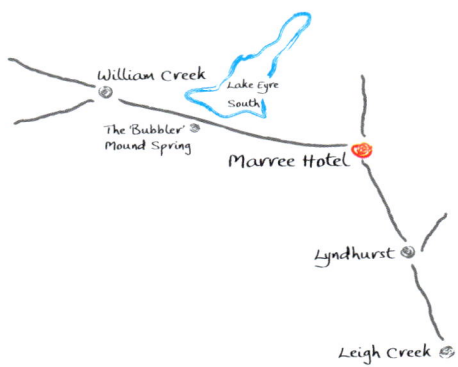

Early records show that this impressive sandstone building was 83 feet by 46 feet with a bar room of 19 feet by 22 feet and a dining room of 17 feet. It would have been quite an impressive public house in little more than a shanty settlement fringing the edge of the desert!

Located directly opposite the old railway station, The Great Northern Hotel, as it was originally known, was built to provide food and lodgings for travellers undertaking the once perilous railway journey on the Old Ghan and drovers moving cattle along the infamous Birdsville Track.

Hergott Springs was the original name given to the area after David Herrgott, a German botanist, who discovered the artesian springs nearby in 1859 whilst on an expedition with explorer John McDouall Stuart. In 1918, with anti-German sentiments having been rife during World War I, the name was officially changed to Marree.

In February 1884 the Central Australian Railway from Port Augusta was extended to Marree. This strategically positioned railhead then allowed for livestock from northern Queensland to be brought down the Birdsville Track and then transported to the Adelaide markets by rail. It wasn't long before the town's population boasted some 600 people along with numerous businesses.

In the early 1920s, when droving was in full swing, it wasn't uncommon for up to 20,000 mixed head of both sheep and cattle to be brought down the Birdsville Track each season 'on the hoof' to be railed out of Marree.

Birdsville, Innamincka, Oodnadatta, repeater stations on the Telegraph Line and other far-flung destinations, received their goods from Marree via camel trains. Imported from countries such as Egypt, Turkey and Persia, these beasts of burden were utilised for all sorts of jobs, carrying wool, farming and fencing goods along with building materials for the Overland Telegraph and the railway as it pushed towards Oodnadatta and eventually to Alice Springs. The men who were skilled in handling these camel strings, although not necessarily from Afghanistan, became known as Afghans or Ghans.

By 1910 there were over 60 cameleers and 1500 camels working out of Marree. As a lasting tribute to these men and their camels the railway became known as 'The Ghan'. Camel transport had all but ended by the late 1930s.

Marree's decline commenced when motorised road trains were introduced for transportation of livestock. Droving ceased along the Birdsville Track in the 1960s, then in 1980 the last train ran along The Ghan railway line.

These days Marree is a popular break for travellers exploring the historic Birdsville and Oodnadatta tracks, Lake Eyre and the Simpson Desert.

Dating from 1883, this grand two storey hotel seems out of place in present day Marree where most of the town's buildings are simple corrugated iron structures.

MIDDLETON HOTEL

Middleton, which consists of the pub and a ramshackle public hall, was once described as 'a desperately lonely tin shelter sharing a desolate landscape with two petrified tree trunks'.

Middleton Hotel
Kennedy Developmental Road, Middleton
Queensland
(07) 4657 3980

Built in 1876 by a carrier named Wiggins, the Middleton Hotel was the first of eight hotels to be built along the Boulia-Winton Road. Established during the heady times of Cobb & Co when there was a flurry of transport through these outback regions, the Middleton Hotel is the only surviving hotel along this stretch of road. The pub was used as a coaching station from 1893 until 1915.

Constructed of weatherboards with a corrugated iron roof, the Middleton Hotel is one of the few remaining intact examples of a western Queensland roadside inn, having been altered little over the years. It's a charming building sitting proudly on a vast black soil plain, the seemingly endless horizon only punctuated by scattered flat-topped rocky outcrops and the occasional stunted tree.

Frederick Henderson was granted the first licence for the hotel in 1889, and it has been licenced ever since. Over the years the hotel has been a meeting point for families from the surrounding properties, truckies, graziers, drovers, travellers, council workers and road crews.

The hotel is furnished with a traditional deep verandah and double opening doors to the interior. Inside the bar you'll find photos and stories, on the walls, of the Cobb & Co times as well as snippets of the region's early pastoral history. Out the front of the hotel is an original Cobb & Co coach. This coach was once pulled by camels on the Winton to Boulia run. There are even some old wooden hitching posts out the front which you could quite easily picture horses tied to.

Australian Bush Pubs | 145

MINGELA HOTEL

After the original pub was burnt down it was decided to move the old town hall to be the pub. It was put on logs and rolled forward one block to its current location.

Mingela Hotel
Hervey Street, Mingela
Queensland
(07) 4770 3106

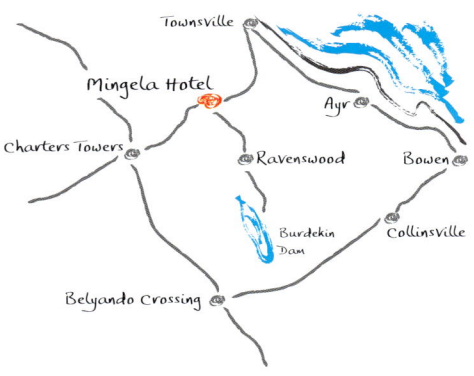

First going by the name of Cunningham in honour of one of the first Europeans to pass through the area in 1861, the town has gone by different names on three separate occasions since its inception in 1881. Just a few short years later the town of Cunningham was seen as the ideal location for a railway junction on the new Townsville - Charters Towers line when it opened in 1882. Two years later in 1884 the town's name was changed to Ravenswood Junction when a branch line to Ravenswood was completed. When the railway line to Ravenswood closed in 1930 the name changed to Mingela, a corruption of the original Aboriginal name 'Ming-illa', meaning big waterhole.

Originally built in 1894 as the two storey North Australian Hotel, the pub enjoyed a steady trade until a fire in 1942 razed the building. The locals, keen to have a pub back up and running, decided that the best course of action would be to repurpose the town's hall as a hotel. The hall was dutifully jacked up and logs placed under it. It was then rolled, on the logs, one full town block to its current position. The front bar and kitchen are the original town hall, with additions to the current building having been added over the years.

The pub's name changed in the mid 1980s from the North Australian Hotel to the Mingela Hotel.

Before the coming of the railway the town was once an important stop for stage coaches undertaking the four day trip from Charters Towers to Townsville. Today, Mingela is a popular 'Sunday drive' destination from the coast.

Australian Bush Pubs | 149

NERRIGA HOTEL

After a dubious start as a sly grog shop and a number of interesting name changes, the Nerriga Hotel, between Nowra and Braidwood, is still dispensing refreshments to the travelling public.

Nerriga Hotel
Braidwood Road, Nerriga
New South Wales
(02) 4845 9120

In the mid 1800s James Dunn established an illegal drinking house in the newly discovered Nerriga goldfields, but it wasn't until 1864 that the premises were officially opened as the Cricketers' Arms Hotel. Later its name was changed to the Commercial Hotel and a century after becoming licenced, in 1966, new ownership instigated yet another name change, this time to the rather intriguing Bark Tree Pub. Today, this charming single storey weatherboard and corrugated iron highland's establishment goes by the relatively straightforward name of Nerriga Hotel.

The small village of Nerriga is located high up in the coastal escarpment country along the Braidwood-Nowra Road. The road, originally known as the 'Wool Road' and built in 1841 by convict labour, saw Nerriga became an important stopover point for teamsters carting wool and other produce from Goulburn and the Monaro region to the port on Jervis Bay bound for Sydney.

Then, in 1851 after alluvial gold was discovered on the Shoalhaven River, the area grew as prospectors flocked to the new diggings. Records show that between 1878 and 1902 over 14 100 ounces of gold were taken from the area.

Today's Nerriga is a far cry from its boisterous past. There are a few houses, a museum, and the hotel. Along with the born and bred locals, the many 'new settlers' who have escaped the city rat-race, add to the mix of characters you're likely to meet at the bar.

Australian Bush Pubs | 151

NINDIGULLY PUB

This rambling old bush pub on the banks of the Moonie River has long held an enviable reputation for conviviality with both locals and travellers since its early days as a coach changing station.

Nindigully Pub
Sternes Street, Nindigully
Queensland
(07) 4625 9637

Nindigully Pub is an imposing wooden building with a wide wrap-around verandah and shady beer garden. Set in a picturesque location, it looks out over the tree-lined Moonie River.

Established in 1864, it is said that the building was originally shearer's quarters on Nindigully Station prior to becoming a coach changing station and then a pub. It is believed the hotel, which is still in its original location, holds the longest continual licence in Queensland.

Inside, the pub is bursting with character. There's a main bar with the now almost obligatory hat collection on the wall, saddles, posters, the skin of a 'Nindigully Geko', mounted animal heads and various curios from around the district. There's also an interesting assortment of framed newspaper and magazine tear sheets adorning one of the walls. The bar counter tops are massive timber slabs while the original rough-sawn timber floorboards on the verandah add to the pub's rustic appeal. A delightful timber lined dining room is just off the bar, and it too has many black and white photographs on the walls from the town's heyday.

In 1862 a once-weekly mail run commenced from Surat, running south to Mungindi on the New South Wales/Queensland border. It followed the Balonne River through St George to Nindigully. At Nindigully the route crossed the Moonie River prior to continuing on to Mungindi. This route was also used by cattlemen droving stock north from New South Wales into Queensland's newly settled western downs.

With the increase of stock movements and the population growth in the early 1860s, as people pushed up from the south, there came a need for commercial premises to supply the necessary services of food and accommodation.

The first of the region's hotels appeared in Mungindi and St George, with Nindigully being the next locale to be issued a licence for a hotel. In September 1864 Thomas Bradford became publican of the aptly named Nindigully Hotel.

As the use of the route from Mungindi to St George continued to flourish, a timber bridge was constructed in 1885 to cross the Moonie River. Although no longer in use, the old bridge still spans the river opposite the hotel.

The licence changed to James Roger in June 1876 and the name changed to the Travellers Rest Hotel. After this time there were three more name changes, including The Sportsmans Arms, before it reverted to its original name of Nindigully Hotel. There have been a total of 25 licensees of the hotel since Thomas Bradford.

These days the main road bypasses Nindigully, which is made up of the pub, a couple of houses, the old General Store and a town hall. The town's permanent population is six!

New Year's Eve is one of the biggest nights of the year in Nindigully with people coming from far and wide to join in the celebrations.

Australian Bush Pubs | 159

NOCCUNDRA HOTEL

Noccundra Hotel was established to serve thirsty station workers from surrounding pastoral stations, as well as teamsters carting supplies and drovers plying the southern stock routes.

Noccundra Hotel
Wilson Street, Noccundra
Queensland
(07) 4655 4317

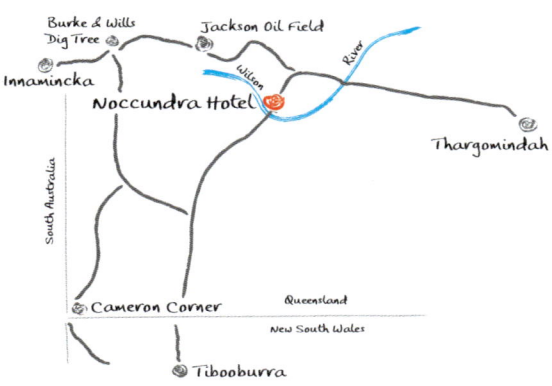

It is believed the current Noccundra Hotel replaced an earlier rough shanty pub which traded on the site from about the late 1860s, around the time of the establishment of Nockatunga Station.

Located opposite a permanent waterhole on the Wilson River, Noccundra was at the intersection of stock routes south to Tibooburra in New South Wales and west into South Australia on the Cooper Creek. It soon became a well received resting place for drovers to spell stock.

There are no records as to who built the present building, but James Gardiner held the first licence from 1883. The handsome, single storey sandstone building, which comprises of a bar room with an adjacent dining room, complete with open fire, is heritage listed.

A town reserve was created in 1885 and by the end of 1889 consisted of a store and police station, along with the hotel.

Henry Hughes, the then owner of Nockatunga Station, purchased both the store and hotel in 1915. The store traded up until 1933, and then in 1959 the police station closed. The township of Noccundra never really eventuated, although the hotel has continued to trade since being licenced, serving stockmen, workers from the surrounding gas and oil fields as well as travellers.

The hotel stayed in the ownership of the Hughes family until 1991, when Nockatunga Station, along with the hotel — which is on land owned by Nockatunga — was purchased by the Packer family's Australian Consolidated Pastoral Co.

Looking for Leichhardt

In 1848 the wiley Prussian-born explorer Ludwig Leichhardt and his party vanished without trace somewhere in northern Australia in an attempt to traverse Australia from east to west. Leichhardt was an experienced bushman and navigator. The disappearance of the fully provisioned party still remains a mystery. They were last seen at Cogoon Station near Roma.

In 1874 Andrew Hume, following a stint in Parramatta Goal for robbery, set off in search of Leichhardt. Hume claimed that in 1862 he had met one of the exploring party, a man by the name of Classen, living with Aboriginals in the Victoria River area of northern Australia. Hume said he was unable to persuade the white man, who was in possession of papers proving his identity, to come with them.

Timothy O'Hea and Lewis Thompson joined the party after other men had pulled out, and along with Hume headed for Cooper Creek en route to Victoria River. At Nockatunga Station on the Wilson River, near Noccundra, Hume and his group took a wrong turn, taking them into the rugged foothills of the Grey Range, away from water. While Thompson found his way back to a creek, both Hume and O'Hea perished from thirst.

A monument to Hume and his party is located at the hotel.

Along with Thompson and O'Hea, Hume became embattled in a struggle for survival to the west of remote Nockatunga Station.

164 | *Australian Bush Pubs*

OASIS ROADHOUSE

Perched beside the Kennedy Developmental Road at Lynd Junction, this welcoming roadhouse boasts Australia's smallest bar where you're likely to rub shoulders with both locals and travellers alike.

Oasis Roadhouse
Kennedy Developmental Road, Lynd Junction
Queensland
(07) 4062 5291

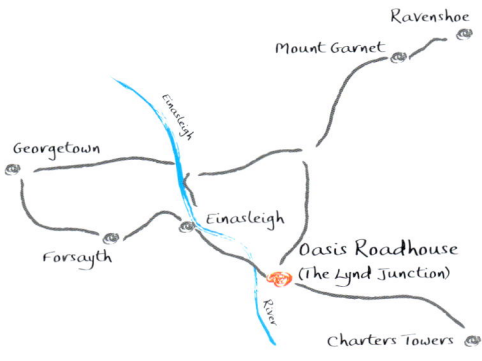

The Lynd Junction is the meeting point of four of north Queensland's major road routes. This alone makes it a top spot for a roadhouse and somewhere for travellers to break their journey. In addition, the Oasis also boasts the smallest bar in Australia. At just 144cm by 134 cm it's just big enough to swing the proverbial cat. As they say, two's company and three's a crowd and this certainly holds true at the Oasis.

Started as a Roadhouse in the 1950s, the Oasis marked the halfway point on the then arduous overland trip from Hughenden to Cairns. The original proprietor used the site to store 44 gallon fuel drums which he dropped off here for refuelling his truck when carting cattle to the meat works in Cairns. With time a shop was eventually added in the late 60s. It was a pretty basic affair by all accounts comprising of just a kerosene fridge stocked with soft drinks and some snacks.

A license was added sometime around 1980, and as they say, the rest is history.

Surrounded by vast cattle stations, the Oasis is a magnet to locals who come in for a bit of rest and relaxation, along with truckies and travellers who ply the long, lonely roads in this part of the country.

Fringed by palm trees, this neat and friendly establishment offers up a somewhat tropical feel, far removed from its rather barren surrounds, which is typical of this savannah landscape.

Apart from the quirky little bar, the roadhouse offers up meals and there is accommodation and camping out the back.

Australian Bush Pubs | 169

OVERLAND CORNER HOTEL

This classic colonial inn, reputedly the oldest surviving hotel to be built along the Murray River, has had a colourful past, hosting patrons ranging from bushrangers to ghosts.

Overland Corner Hotel
Old Coach Road, Overland Corner
South Australia
(08) 7552 5660

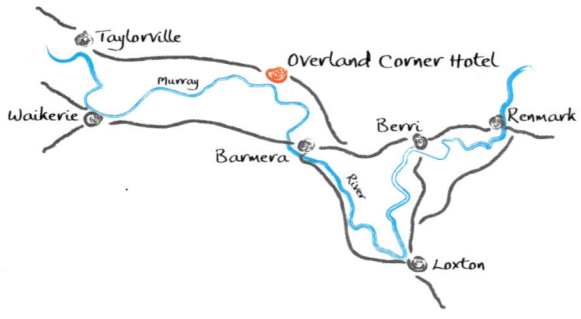

The Overland Corner Hotel was built by the Brand brothers in 1859 for pastoralist, John Chambers. Using local materials, it was constructed of limestone blocks hewn from a nearby quarry, local red gum and native Murray pine timbers and a thatched roof of river reeds. One of the brothers, William, was the hotel's first licensee.

The hotel originally sat on land which was part of Chambers' Cobdogla Station, a sprawling cattle property on the Murray River. The 'overland corner' refers to the river bend where large mobs of cattle were swum across the river after drovers had moved them 'overland' from New South Wales, destined for the Adelaide markets. The extensive river flat below the hotel was used as a holding paddock for stock, while no doubt, many a drover enjoyed the pub's hospitality. Today it's a popular camping area.

The pub operated for almost 40 years before being delicenced in 1897. It operated as a store and post office until 1965 when the property was bought by the National Trust and restored. It was relicenced as a hotel in 1987. Having withstood plenty of floods, fires and other natural disasters, the hotel was taken over and brought back to its former glory by Brad and Nicole Flowers.

Like most good pubs, The Overland Corner Hotel is not without a swag of yarns. Irishman Andrew Scott, otherwise known as bushranger Captain Moonlight, is alleged to have had a drink or two at the hotel with a few accomplices. Moonlight is said to have rode his horse into the front bar. Ghosts of past patrons are also said to still enjoy the pub's hospitality, revelling into the early hours, long after the lights are out!

Australian Bush Pubs | 175

PRAIRIE HOTEL

The Prairie hosts a fascinating and rather eclectic collection of local memorabilia which the current publicans have collected over the years. This alone makes this friendly pub worth a visit.

**Prairie Hotel
Flinders Highway, Prairie
Queensland
(07) 4741 5121**

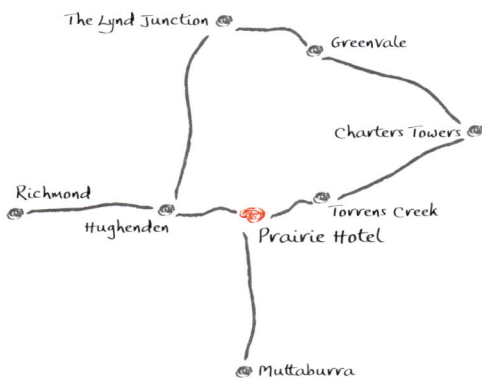

Taking its name from the flat, featureless grasslands of America's wild west, Australia's very own Prairie can trace its beginnings to the days of stage coach travel when a horse changing station was established here by Cobb & Co in 1868. The town grew as squatters moved sheep onto the area's vast Flinders Grass plains. A shearing shed was soon built on the outskirts of town where squatters would drive their sheep for shearing. This was before properties had their own facilities.

In its heyday Prairie had a couple of hotels, guest houses and general stores along with a school, baker, butcher, saddler and a private dance hall in addition to other essential businesses. During the early 1900s the town had a population of 300 people. Today about 50 people call Prairie home.

The Prairie is the sole remaining hostelry of the two which once existed in the town. Serving stage coach services, and later railway passengers when the line reached town in 1887, the pub is also said to have been frequented by the legendary Harry Readford, alias Captain Starlight, who is best known for his daring cattle duffing exploits. The pub is now a focal point for both locals and travellers.

Current publicans, Andrea and Tom Duddy, have spent years amassing an outstanding stash of collectibles and curios from the surrounding area and these adorn the walls and nooks and crannies of the pub. The front bar hosts an old dentist's chair where you can sip your beer while the pub's dining room will take you back to a more genteel time.

Australian Bush Pubs | 179

The Roaming Ringer

The Prairie's resident ghost is said to be that of a ringer (stockman) who died in a fire sometime in the 1930s. Local folklore tells the story that the then owner of the Prairie Hotel offered the ringer a down payment of a bottle of overproof rum to burn the town's newly installed opposing hotel. The ringer was then, as final payment, to receive a gold sovereign from the publican when the job was done.

Drinking in the bar of the competing pub for much of the night, the ringer, when hearing the call for last drinks, duly wandered off and concealed himself in one of the guest rooms. To while away the time he fortified himself with a few tokes from his rum bottle. When the coast was clear he snuck into the pub's kitchen, setting fire to the place. He then retreated back to his hiding place to retrieve his rum bottle, opportunistically had a few more swigs and then, being quite inebriated, fell asleep. The ringer perished in the fire which razed the pub to the ground.

It is said that the ringer now prowls the Prairie seeking his payment of a gold sovereign. Coincidentally, the pub's front bar is known as 'The Old Ringer's Bar'.

With a down payment of a bottle of OP rum and the promise of a gold sovereign, the ringer was enlisted to burn down the opposing pub.

ROYAL HOTEL – BEDOURIE

Bedourie is situated in the south-west corner of Queensland on a vast gibber strewn plain and surrounded by sandhills. The sole remaining pub, the Royal, has served the town continuously since 1886.

Royal Hotel
Herbert Street, Bedourie
Queensland
(07) 4746 1201

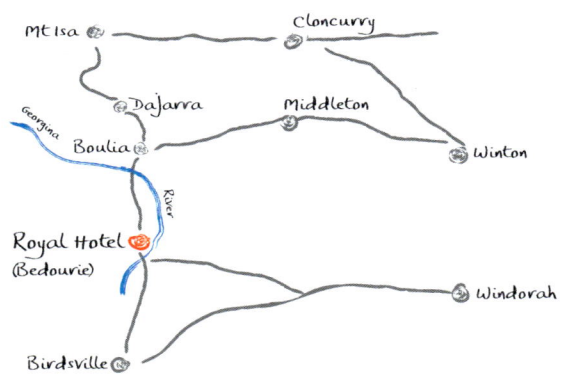

Bedourie grew from a shanty settlement located on the main north-south stock route which linked stations in the north of Queensland and the Northern Territory to Marree in South Australia.

Of the town's two hotels, The Royal was built sometime during 1886 to serve the growing community. It was constructed of kiln-fired mud bricks — as opposed to the more common method of sun drying — a task which took almost two years to complete. The hotel's first licensee was James Craigie, who ran the pub with his wife.

As the 1800s drew to a close, Bedourie had cemented its position as an important supply centre for grazing properties throughout the Channel Country. It had also become a well established stopover for drovers using the Georgina Stock Route. Bedourie is now the administrative centre for the Diamantina Shire.

The Royal Hotel was gutted by fire in the early 1900s, sustaining substantial damage. It was subsequently rebuilt using local stone but retained some of the original brickwork, the thatched roof replaced with corrugated iron. In later years a boundary workers' hut from Ethabuka Spring was added to the hotel and serves as the dining room.

Today, the exterior of the hotel retains a classic bush pub character with its pitched corrugated iron roof, thick masonry walls and large verandah. Inside there is a main bar at one end with an open fireplace built into the opposing wall. There is a dining room in the back section of the hotel.

The Bedourie Oven

Bedourie lends its name to a simple, but ingenious piece of outback cookware, the Bedourie Camp Oven.

During the late 1800s through to the early 1900s, drover's cooks mostly used cast iron camp ovens to cook any matter of fare from the humble damper — a staple in bush camps — to stews and desserts. Cast iron was heavy and awkward to stow and carry on pack horses as well as brittle; it would often crack when dropped.

It is thought that a bagman, 'on the wallaby' during the Great Depression of the 1930s had come to the Bedourie area looking for work. A tin-smith by trade, the bagman set about fashioning flat sided billy cans along with a number of steel camp ovens. These were stocked by Alan Gaffney's pub store in Bedourie and soon became popular with droving outfits as they passed through the area. The practical utensil soon gained the name of the 'Bedourie Oven'.

In 1945 RM Williams had this style of camp oven made of pressed steel and in the 1960s had the item listed in his mail-order catalogue as a Bedourie Camp Oven.

These lightweight, unbreakable spun steel camp ovens — the fitting lid can be used as a frypan — are still in use by bush cooks today.

ROYAL HOTEL – EROMANGA

Famous for being Australia's furthest town from the ocean, Eromanga once boasted three hotels and was on a well-travelled Cobb & Co route until the advent of motorised transport.

Royal Hotel
Deacon Street, Eromanga
Queensland
(07) 4656 4837

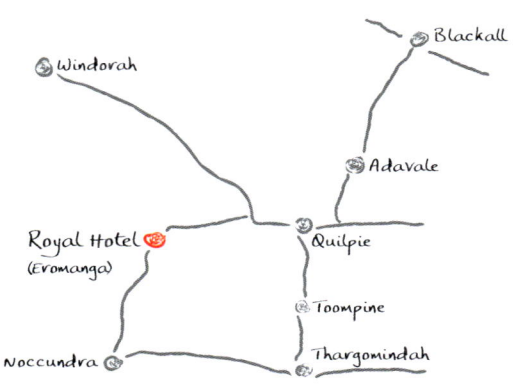

In the early 1870s a settlement by the name of 'Opal Opolis' formed in the locality of a shanty pub popularly called the 'Round House'. Established to service the opal miners at the Little Wonder mines on Mt Margaret Station, in March 1879 the settlement was gazetted as the town of Eromanga, reputedly an Aboriginal word meaning 'Windy Plain'. Even today, the dust swirls around the town as the winds whip in across the sweeping plains from all points of the compass.

At its peak Eromanga supported three hotels, The Royal, The Australian and The Grand. Only the Royal survived and remains open today. First licenced to William McGill in 1886 and constructed of handmade mud bricks, The Royal operated as a Cobb & Co changing station — it was the second last stop on the Kyabra run — as well as being a favoured watering hole for the large shearing teams which regularly passed through the area. Opal buyers coming from the south to purchase the precious stone also used the hotel.

Of the other hotels, The Australian closed its doors in the early 1900s and The Grand was a short lived venture, only being licenced for a few years. In addition to the hotels there were two stores, a school, a police station, a blacksmith shop next to The Royal Hotel and a Chinese market garden beside Euronghoola Creek.

The Royal Hotel is a neat, well kept outback pub. A shady verandah shelters the front while behind the massively thick walls is a cosy front bar with a lounge bar located off to the side.

ROYAL MAIL HOTEL

First licenced in 1874, Hungerford's delightfully charming Royal Mail Hotel has provided refreshments and accommodation to the travelling public for over 140 years.

Royal Mail Hotel
Archernar Street, Hungerford
Queensland
(07) 4655 4093

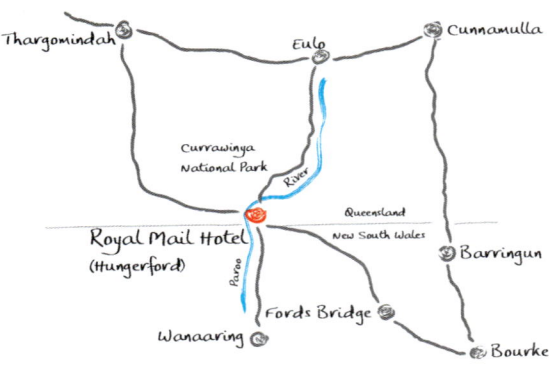

The border township of Hungerford came into being in the early 1870s and was gazetted in 1875. It takes its name from Thomas Hungerford, an Irishman who held substantial grazing properties in the area. Hungerford administered these holdings from his base in the Hunter Valley of New South Wales and often camped beside the Paroo River on his visits to his Queensland properties at a site which became known as 'Hungerford's Camp'.

The Royal Mail Hotel was thought to have been established around the time of the original township and was first licenced in 1874. Another hotel, The Commercial, no longer exists.

Built from timber and corrugated iron, the Royal Mail is practically in original condition — this is one of the few bush pubs with its authentic originality still in tact. There are shady verandahs around two sides, and at the front corner is the doorway into the bar. Wooden floorboards, wood lined walls and a high ceiling, again lined with wood, all add to the atmosphere inside the hotel. Adjoining the front bar is a small dining room with a delightful open fireplace, throughout the pub there are interesting memorabilia on the walls along with snippets about the hotel's history.

The Royal Mail was a changing station for Cobb & Co on the Bourke to Thargomindah/Cunnamulla route. Passengers would have a meal and overnight at the hotel.

Today, the mail contract is still held by the hotel, with the publican delivering mail to the town and surrounding properties.

Henry Lawson's Hungerford

In the sweltering, drought-stricken summer of 1892-93 bush poet Henry Lawson tramped the well-worn track from Bourke to Hungerford in search of stories. He'd been given a train ticket to Bourke and a £5 note by FJ Archibald, editor of the Bulletin magazine, to head bush in search of work and to send back copy for the magazine.

Lawson later wrote in *Hungerford*, one of a collection of stories published in *While the Billy Boils*, 'Hungerford consists of two houses and a humpy in New South Wales and five houses in Queensland. Characteristically enough, both the pubs are in Queensland. We got a glass of sour yeast at one and paid sixpence for it — we had asked for English ale. The Post Office is in New South Wales, and the police-barracks in Bananaland. The police cannot do anything if there is a row going on across the street in New South Wales, except send to Brisbane and have an extradition warrant applied for; and they don't do much if there is a row in Queensland. Most of the rows are across the border in Queensland, where the pubs are.'

Unimpressed by the place, Lawson went on to write 'Next morning we rolled up our swags and left Hungerford to the North-West'.

Lawson vowed 'never to face the bush again' and returned to Sydney.

The pub's underground cellar still exists with shelves dug from the earth on which the wooden kegs of beer would have been stored.

SILVERTON HOTEL

Australia's most photographed pub, the Silverton Hotel has appeared in countless TV commercials as well as box office block-busters like Mad Max II, but despite the fame, it's still a top outback boozer.

Silverton Hotel
Layard Street, Silverton
New South Wales
(08) 8088 5313

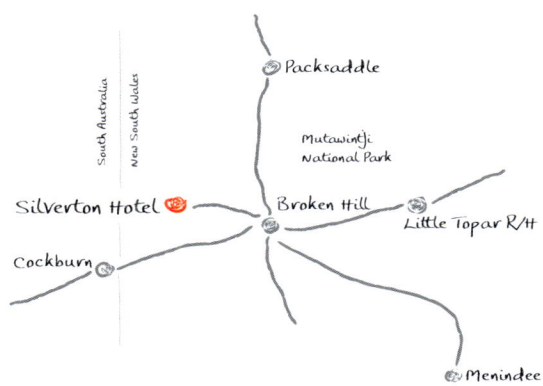

Once a mining town, Silverton — which is a little over 20 kilometres north-west of Broken Hill — is pretty much famous for its pub. Along with a few houses, a couple of churches and an old gaol, there is a small colony of painters and other artisans, many with galleries open to the public, displaying their wares.

The current Silverton Hotel was built in 1885 and is the last remaining of ten licenced premises which serviced, what was then, Australia's richest silver field. At its peak the town had three breweries, one of which was operated by Emil Resch who afterwards founded Resch's Brewery in Sydney.

Over the years there have been three hotels in town going by the name of Silverton Hotel. The first was the De Baun Silverton Hotel — a single storey building built in April 1883. The next was a two storey building erected in 1884, while the current building dates from 1885. Interestingly, all three buildings were built alongside each other.

They must have been a thirsty lot at Silverton back in the 1880s. Local records suggest that when John De Baun swung open the pub's doors for the first time, the drinkers poured nineteen tons of beer down their parched throats in the hotel's first four weeks of operation!

The pub is still essentially a drinking spot for locals and tourists. Constructed from stone and brick with an iron roof, it's a solid looking structure. Inside there is a large bar room with an open fire down one end and scattered around the walls is a collection of memorabilia.

Hollywood of the Outback

Estimated to having been viewed by 500 million people throughout the world, The Silverton Hotel has featured in a string of television series and successful films including: *Wake in Fright*, *The Golden Soak*, *A Town Like Alice*, *Mad Max II* starring Mel Gibson, *Hostage*, *Razorback*, *Blue Lightning*, *Ricky and Pete*, *Dirty Deeds* and Jimeoin's *The Craic*.

The variety of scenery close to town, along with the similarity of the region to other locations in more remote parts of Australia are major factors in Silverton's popularity with film-makers. Add to this the availability of accommodation for large film crews and access to building materials for set construction in nearby Broken Hill, and of course, the bright, sunny weather conditions throughout the year, and you have an ideal cinematographic location.

Over the years the pub has been used by film-makers as a hotel, American diner and coffee shops. The pub has 'appeared' as the Nullagine Hotel in *The Golden Soak*, Hotel Australia in *A Town Like Alice*, Mulga Mulga Hotel in numerous XXXX beer commercials, the Dingo Hotel in *As Time Goes By*, Chuck's Diner in an Eveready Battery commercial, the Mundi Mundi Hotel for a Carling beer commercial and Federal Hotel in the movie *Dirty Deeds*.

... where men outnumbered women by 50 to 1 — the miners sought solace at the bars and hotels which appeared like magic in dry, dusty Silverton.

Australian Bush Pubs

SOFALA ROYAL HOTEL

Sofala is Australia's oldest remaining gold town, dating from 1851. The village's narrow streets house an array of unique period buildings, including the charming Sofala Royal Hotel.

**Sofala Royal Hotel
Denison Street, Sofala
New South Wales
(02) 6337 7008**

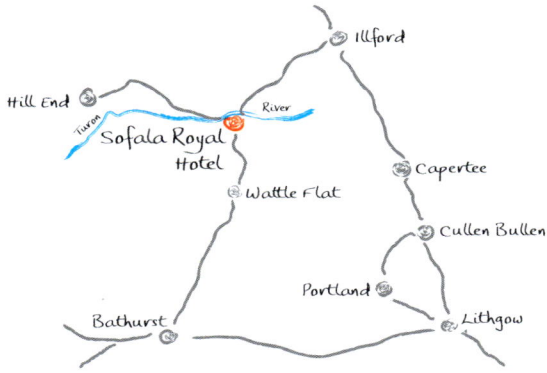

Following the discovery of gold on the Turon River in 1851, a frenetic rush to the area soon saw the establishment of the settlement of Sofala. Set amongst the expanding alluvial workings, this early township, which consisted mostly of canvas tents and bark huts, was spread out along the river west for five kilometres to Wallaby Rocks and a similar distance to the east to Upper Turon. Before long churches, schools, a court of petty sessions, a hospital and many other businesses sprang into existence, servicing this fast growing area.

At the height of gold fever in the mid 1860s there were 50 licenced hotels — although most would have been little more than two roomed shacks — on the fields, along with an estimated 500 illegal sly grog shanties serving the population which was thought to number over 30 000 European diggers and 10 000 Chinese prospectors, all searching for their fortune. The village benefited from its position on the main road between Bathurst and the Hunter region, and the fact that the gold lasted much longer than in many other regions.

Of all the town's pubs, only the Sofala Royal Hotel remains licenced. The two storey weatherboard pub with its impressive wrought-iron balcony, opened at the height of the rush and has traded continuously since becoming first licenced in 1862, except for a brief period in 1940. A number of other hotels are now private dwellings.

The hotel's first proprietor was European immigrant Moritz Mendel and his wife Anne. Anne died during childbirth in 1877 and Moritz is said to have committed suicide in the hotel — five years after the death of his wife and child — in room 6, which is now used as a guestroom. Moritz must have found solace by his own hand as there are no reports that he haunts the hotel after all these years.

Like many hotels of this era, it has a connection to the famous Cobb & Co. The far end of the bar, which is in use today, was once part of a coach booking office. There were regular daily coach services to and from Bathurst as well as a service north to Mudgee and beyond.

As the gold began to peter out the miners and their families moved to other fields — a new strike at Wattle Flat attracted a lot of Sofala's population while others flocked to new finds at Palmers Oaky and Spring Creek. By the early 1870s Sofala's population had declined markedly, although the town managed to survive despite the exodus.

Mining, mostly by large, well funded ventures — including dredges on the Turon River — continued in the area until just before World War I, with sporadic small-scale bursts up until the 1950s.

These days Sofala offers a window into the past. The hotel remains much the same as it would have been during the town's heyday, and is one of the few licenced goldfields pubs from this early time still serving thirsty visitors.

In 1986 floodwaters from the swollen Turon River inundated the hotel, but luckily they receded quickly, saving the hotel's bottom storey from ruin.

SOUTH WESTERN HOTEL

Once a welcome respite for local graziers, opal miners and travelling shearing teams — many of them on pushbikes — along the Quilpie to Thargomindah road, the 'Toompine Pub' is a still popular venue today.

**South Western Hotel
Stanley Street, Toompine
Queensland
(07) 4656 4721**

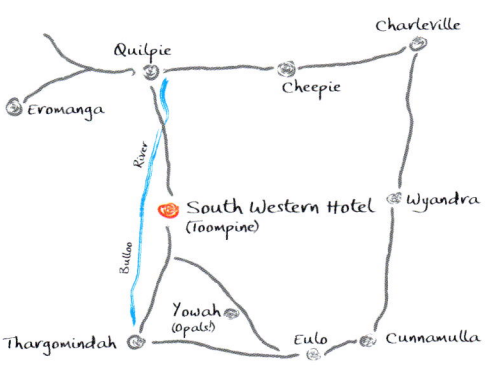

Established in the 1860s, this little western Queensland pub on the Cobb & Co run from Thargomindah to Adavale, is where passengers overnighted and horses were changed. As time went by a small community formed, with the pub becoming a popular drinking spot for station hands, opal miners and shearing teams. It is now a well regarded stopover with travellers. The name Toompine is thought to have come from the Aboriginal 'thuenpin', meaning leech.

All that now remains, along with a hall, is the South Western Hotel, generally known as 'The Toompine Pub'. This is the second pub to stand on this site; the first hotel was destroyed by fire. The present hotel was built in 1893 by Mr Power and constructed of cypress pine and ripple iron.

The first known publican at Toompine was John Webber of Kyabra Station. Webber was also a partner in the Peppin Opal Mine. There are suggestions that Webber built the first hotel, although by 1866 a Mrs Scanlan is recorded as being the owner.

The early 1900s opal boom saw hundreds of miners flocking to the Duck Creek and Copperella fields. The only pub in a hundred miles to spend their new won fortunes was at Toompine, and no doubt they did a roaring trade. It was at Duck Creek that Queensland's largest opal the 'Huns Head' was found in 1972, weighing in at 15.75kg.

The South Western has received some renovations and extensions over the last few years, but still retains much of its former character.

The current owners' great aunt, Eileen McNamara, was the proprietor from 1940 (roughly when this photograph, on the right, was taken) to 1970. The lamp post in the picture near the horse was the Cobb & Co light. This light remains with one of the family members today. People that lived and worked nearby often rode in on horseback.

SURVEYOR GENERAL INN

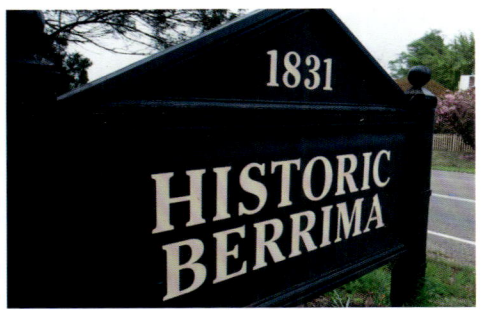

This beautiful old pub, which wouldn't look out of place in the Cotwolds of England, is the centrepiece of Berrima, an almost equally quaint village. The inn lays claim to being the oldest continuously licensed pub in Australia.

**Surveyor General Inn
Old Hume Highway, Berrima
New South Wales
Ph (02) 4877 1226**

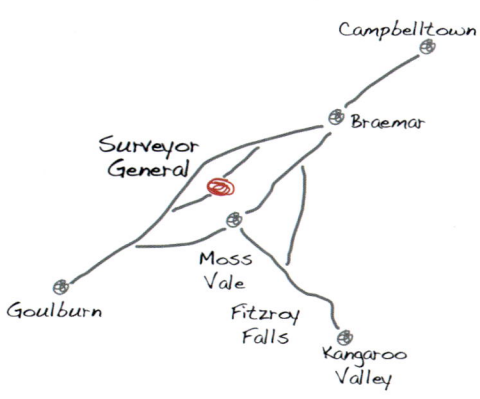

The Surveyor General Inn is the last remaining hotel in the historic village of Berrima in the southern highlands of NSW and is Australia's oldest continuously licensed inn. Berrima was once a far more bustling town, boasting four hotels, a courthouse, gaol and other public buildings. It was a popular stop-off for Cobb & Co Coaches to and from Sydney. All this in turn made the town a popular haunt for bushrangers.

The two-storey Surveyor General was built of convict-hewn sandstone, quarried from nearby, in 1834 for James Harper. The Harper family owned the inn for close to a century. The cellar was used to lock-up convicts until the goal was built a few years later.

The Surveyor General has seen a few changes over its long lifespan. One of these, in the 1890s, was the addition of an upper storey balcony running the length of the building (it has now been removed). By the 1960s the Surveyor General's condition had declined so badly that plans were afoot to knock it down. Fortunately, a group of people raised enough funds for many of the important buildings in Berrima, including the Surveyor General, to be restored.

The hotel now boasts many of its original features and the historic main bar radiates a comfortable ambience within its stone walls, timber and pressed metal ceilings, carved cedar bar and open fireplace. This is not an establishment frozen in time. Along with the old-world charm, visitors will find a welcoming beer garden and alfresco dining.

THE DANGI PUB

This friendly bush pub, south-west of Mt Isa, was once a haunt for Georgina Stock Route drovers, and for those willing to venture off the beaten track it offers a taste of the 'real' Queensland outback.

The Dangi Pub
Main Street, Urandangi
Queensland
(07) 4748 4988

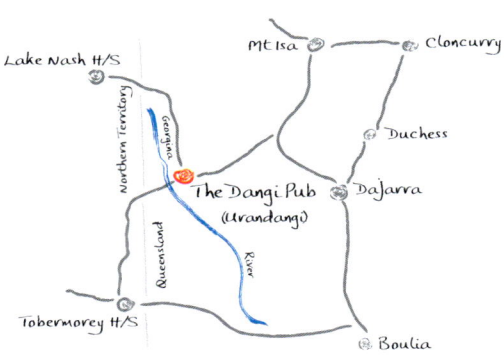

At one time the small settlement of Urandangi was an important rest stop along the Georgina Stock Route, and the hotel was one of the most popular with droving plants who brought thousands of head of cattle down from the Barkly Tableland. The droving days are long gone and the town now exists in quieter times.

Urandangi was founded by James Hutton and Charles Webster, who set up as storekeepers in this remote outpost in 1885 to service the trade along the stock route. Today the store is closed, but the Urandangi Hotel, or 'The Dangi Pub' as it is known to most, survives, and along with a few houses, makes up the town.

Located on the edge of a sweeping plain and not far from the Georgina River channels, the settlement has an almost quintessential remoteness which typifies far western Queensland.

The original pub burned to the ground in 1932, but was soon replaced when the old hospital building from Kuridala was relocated some 130 kilometres — as the crow flys — to Urandangi after the former tin mining town, located to the south of Cloncurry, was abandoned.

The Dangi Pub is a great example of north western Queensland vernacular building style. Constructed of timber with a corrugated iron roof, it has a wide, shady verandah all around. Inside, the original floorboards add a depth of character to the hotel which consists of a timber lined bar room and a dining room. There is a tree shaded beer garden out the back.

At the time of writing this third edition, The Dangi Pub was closed due to extensive flood damage. However the proprietors are hopeful to reopen the doors soon.

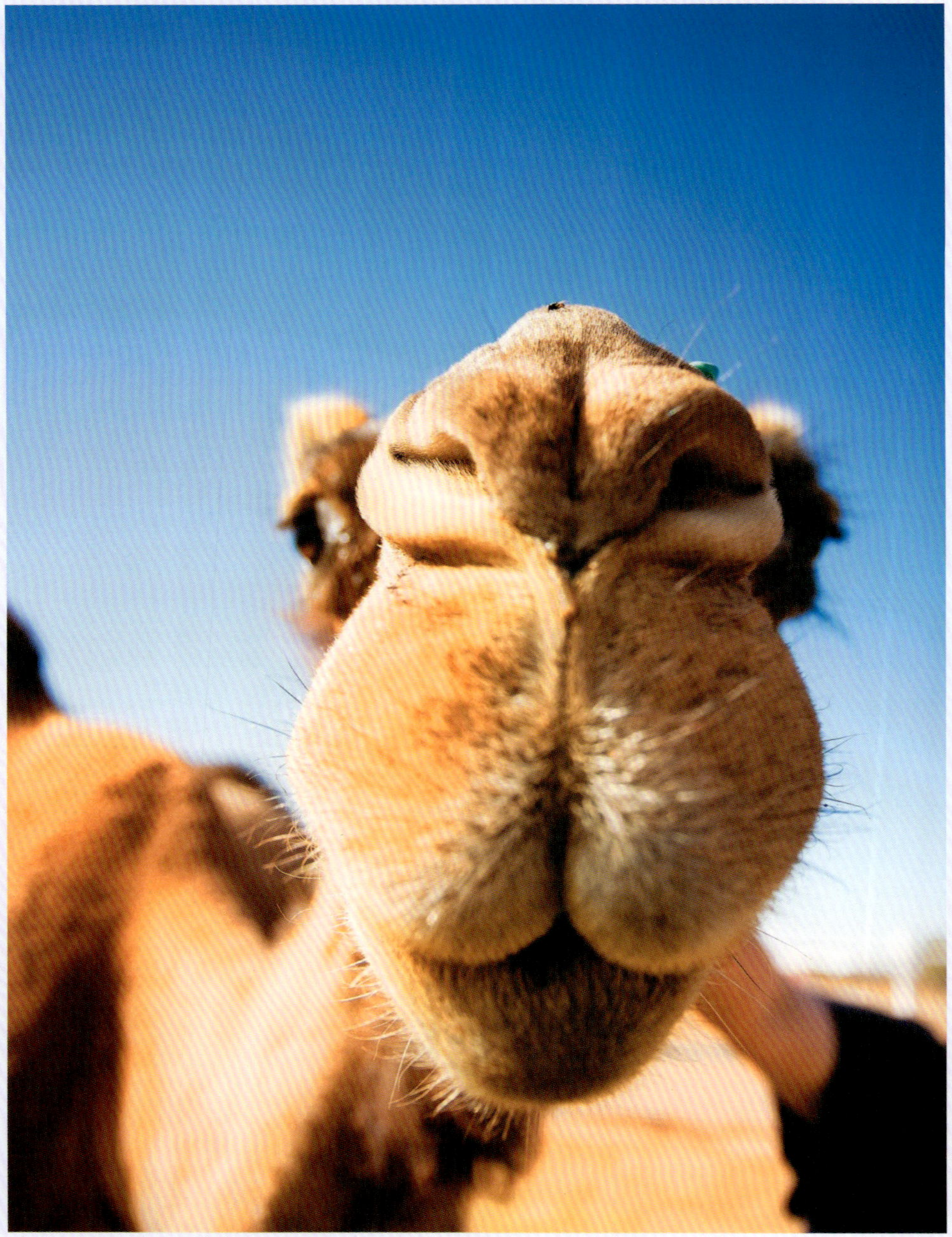

CASTLEMAINE
XXXX
GOLD

URANDAN

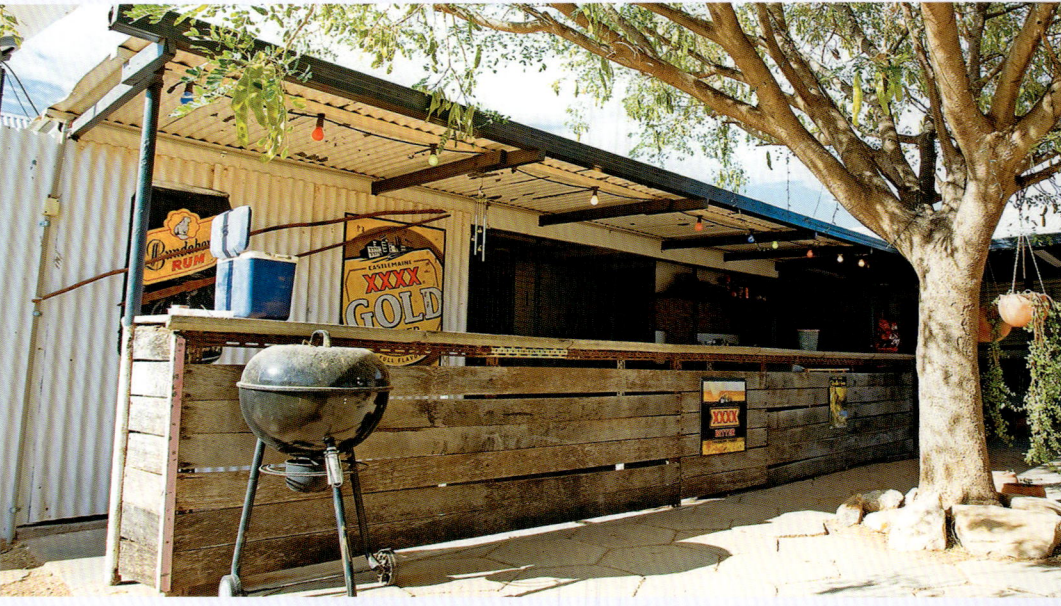

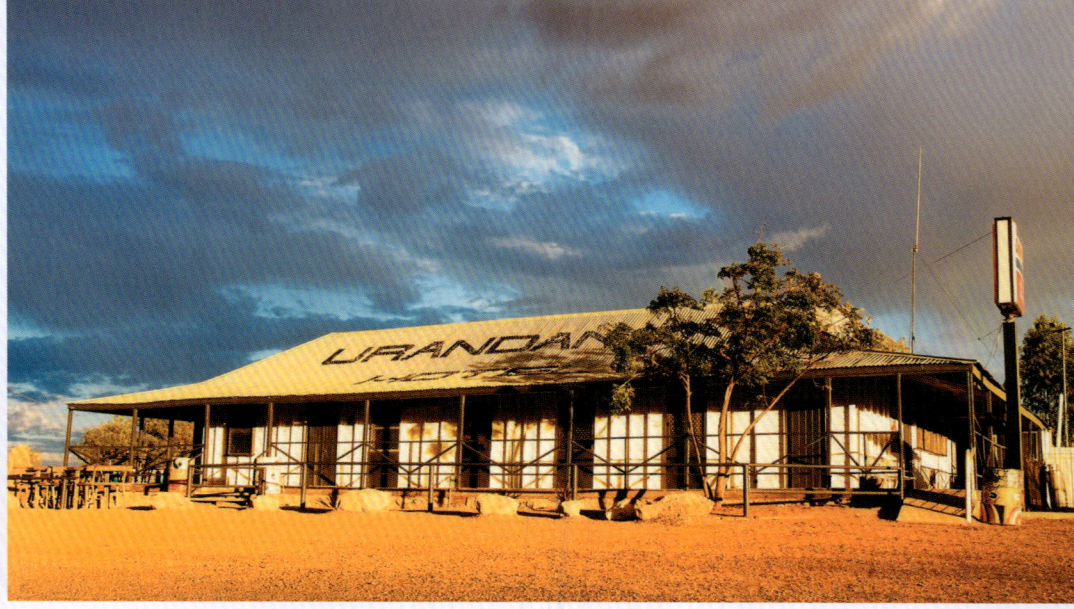

THE FAMILY HOTEL

Sited in a strikingly arid landscape, Tibooburra frequently registers the highest temperatures in New South Wales. Offering welcome relief for thirsty locals and travellers is The Family Hotel.

**The Family Hotel
Briscoe Street, Tibooburra
New South Wales
(08) 8091 3314**

Built by Francis Bladen in 1883 of locally quarried sandstone, Tibooburra's Family Hotel is one of two pubs in this remote corner country town. The town's other hotel, The Tibooburra, is generally referred to as the 'Two Storey'.

The Family was once part of the web-like Cobb & Co network where passengers gained respite from the rough and tumble of stage coach travel, and horses were changed for the next leg of the journey. Even today the old horse stables are still located out the back of the pub.

Tibooburra was established at the height of the gold rush. First named 'The Granites' after the ancient granite tors which stand almost fortress-like surrounding the village, Tibooburra was originally part of the Albert Goldfields which was centred around Milparinka, about 40 kilometres to the south. Cattle King Sidney Kidman set up the first ration store on the new goldfield.

Fronting the town's main street with a shady verandah to sit and relax, the hotel is a substantial building, its massive sandstone block walls providing a feeling of permanence. Inside there are two bar rooms, along with a foyer with an open fire. There are a number of other rooms as well.

Adorning the walls of the pub are a collection of original murals painted by well-known artists Clifton Pugh, Russell Drysdale, Max Miller and Ric Amor. All were regular visitors to the corner country — as well as the hotel — being inspired by the region's rugged, desolate landscapes.

Pugh's Pub

Clifton Pugh was one of Australia's best known painters, widely regarded for his expressionist landscapes and portraiture. He was a three-time winner of the Archibald Prize.

During the 1960s and 70s, Pugh, along with other popular artists of the day, spent considerable time at Tibooburra. Pugh also ran painting workshops around the town, using the desert vastness of the area as subjects. It has been said that Tibooburra — but probably more so The Family Hotel — was Pugh's second home!

Pugh owned the The Family Hotel for a period, although he was not the owner of the pub at the time the walls were used by the artists; it was run by Barney Davie, a mate of Pugh's. One story goes that Pugh was stranded at the pub during wet weather. He became bored after awhile and started doodling on the walls. This was in 1969. This no doubt set the scene with Pugh leaving a number of artworks, along with a bacchanalian mural on one of the walls. Pugh also painted a devil with a beard which bore a striking resemblance to his ex-wife's boyfriend. There are also two nude murals who were said to be the pub owner's daughters.

Pugh died in 1990.

... some were painted in exchange for a few beers but when Pugh hit the big time, becoming rich and famous, he ended up buying the pub.

220 | Australian Bush Pubs

THE LOGAN PUB

This Victorian goldfields pub has become a bit of an institution. Standing on the edge of the famous 'Golden Triangle', it's been host to many a fortune seeker over the last century.

The Logan Pub
Wimmera Hwy, Logan
Victoria
(03) 5496 2220

The tiny hamlet of Logan is located in Victoria's famous 'Golden Triangle'. Bordered by the towns of Wedderburn to the north, Dunolly to the south and Inglewood to the east, 'The Triangle' has contributed 90% of the world's largest gold nuggets. Welcome Stranger, the world's largest nugget, was found at Moliagul, near Dunolly, in 1869. Even today valuable nuggets are still being unearthed in the area, making it popular with prospectors.

With the discovery of gold came outlaws. Bushranger Francis McCallum, alias 'Captain Melville' was notorious for his highwayman feats in the area during 1851. Nearby Melville Caves is said to have been used as a hideout by the outlaw, however, he was a little early for a beer as the first pub at Logan wasn't built for another four years!

The weatherboard clad and corrugated iron roofed hotel is the third pub to be sited in Logan, although there has been a pub here since the mid 1850s when gold prospectors converged on the area. The hamlet's first pub was moved to a nearby sheep property and used as shearer's quarters after the grazier bought the pub — he was becoming tired of trying to get his inebriated shearers back to work. Subsequently, a second hotel was built on the site but burnt down. The third and current building was built in 1910.

Inside this friendly little hotel there is a small bar room off to one side while a larger room houses a pool table and a dining room. The walls of the front bar host a collection of odds and ends from axes to pen sketches.

Australian Bush Pubs | 225

THE PUB IN THE PADDOCK

One of Tasmania's oldest country pubs, the St Columba Falls Hotel, is essentially a pub in the middle of a paddock. It was originally a guesthouse for visitors to the falls before becoming a hotel.

St Columba Falls Hotel
St Columba Falls Road, Pyengana
Tasmania
(03) 6373 6121

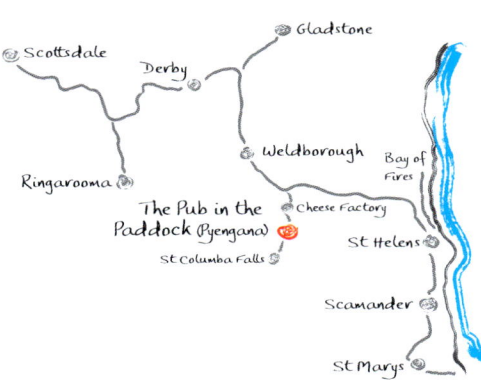

Tucked away in the tranquil Pyengana Valley is the charming St Columba Falls Hotel, otherwise known as The Pub in the Paddock. Apart from a delightful location — within close proximity to St Columba Falls — the hotel boasts a unique resident, Priscilla the beer-drinking pig. Boy, this swine really knows how to drink! She can knock back a stubbie in about four seconds. Even though it's only water with a little bit of added beer slops, it's still an impressive feat.

The heritage-listed pub dates back to the 1880s and some sections of the original structure remain. Built as a residence for the Terry family and their 12 children, the home first operated as a B&B for visitors to the falls before eventually becoming a hotel. It gained its licence in 1901.

The name 'Pub in the Paddock' is said to have originated from mail that was addressed to the hotel in the early days. Many of the senders either didn't know, or couldn't remember, the pub's official title so simply sent letters addressed to 'The Pub in the Paddock'. The name stuck.

The pub itself consists of a cosy timber-lined front bar with the obligatory open fireplace in one corner. This is a popular spot on those chilly Tassie nights. Out the back there is a large dining room — this time with a slow combustion heater — and off this there are a number of accommodation guestrooms. A small verandah is attached to the front of the original entrance way and a grassed area also has seating for those sunny afternoons.

Australian Bush Pubs

Tiger Tales

Pyengana is about 25 kilometres inland from the fishing and holiday town of St Helens. The valley's lush green pastures are home to dairy cattle. There's even a small cheese factory here.

But in 1995 it was a frenzied scene with reporters and journalists converging on the sleepy valley after word spread that a Tasmanian Tiger, believed to have been extinct since the 1930s, had been purportedly sighted by a forestry ranger in a remote area of the valley. There had been a number of sightings of the thylacine here, but this one, coming from a ranger, seemed kosher.

According to the book, *Carnivorous Nights*, the ranger told the Sydney Morning Herald newspaper 'What I viewed for two minutes was about half the size of a fully matured German shepherd dog, he had stripes over his body from about half way down, and his tail was curved like a kangaroo's. ... He sniffed the ground, lifted his head and ran into the bush. He was a scrappy color like a dingo — that horrible sandy color that looks like he needed a bath.'

The sighting was apparently made near the St Columba Falls. Was it a hoax? The book goes on to say that the publican of the day allegedly paid a part-time forestry ranger $500 to say that he had seen the tiger in order to drum up business for the pub, which it did!

In December 1998 a group reported seeing what looked like a 'tiger' on the road between Pyengana and Weldborough.

TILPA HOTEL

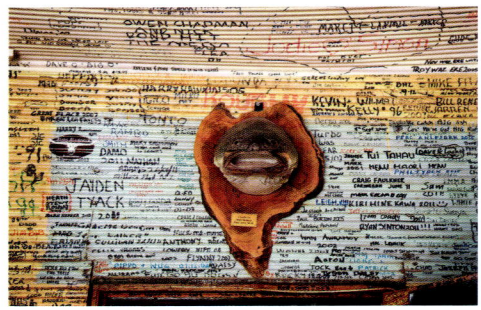

This corrugated iron gem sits on the banks of the Darling River south of Bourke. Just oozing with character, this pub is hard to go past as you wind your way along the famous inland river.

Tilpa Hotel
Darling Street, Tilpa
New South Wales
(02) 6837 3928

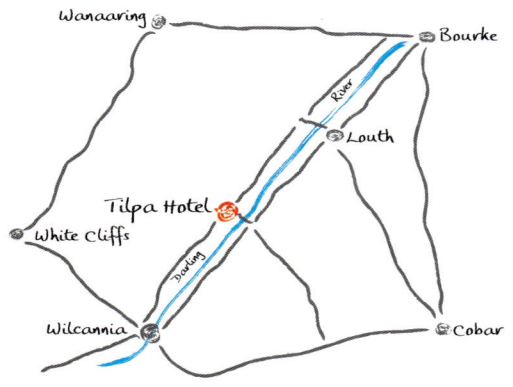

To many, the Tilpa Hotel is considered one of the last remaining true bush pubs. Established in 1894, the hotel grew from the river boat trade that once plied the Darling River. Pastoralism also added buoyancy to the local area, as it still does today. You'll more than likely be rubbing shoulders with cockies, shearers, rouseabouts and wool pressers in the pub's front bar.

Interestingly, the poet Harry 'Breaker' Morant once worked in the area, droving cattle and breaking horses before heading off to the Boer War and into the history books. His name is inscribed on the village's war memorial.

An observation from 1927 described the pub then as 'a wooden building with an iron roof consisting of a main portion containing a first class dining room, 2 parlours, 8 bedrooms and large wire gauze covered sleeping out space, also a detached building consisting of kitchen and second class dining room...'.

Today's Tilpa Hotel has changed little. This humble 100-odd year old attraction, made from corrugated iron and weatherboard with a concrete floor, is a great meeting place. Inside is a front bar and a dining room.

Local characters always have a few stories and tall tales from this part of the world. They may even let you in on the good fishing spots along the river, and if the monster heads of the Murray River Cod which adorn the pub's walls are anything to go by, the fishing here might be well worth a try!

Walls of Graffiti

There aren't too many pubs where you can write your name on the wall with a permanent marker pen, but at the Tilpa Pub you can, and all for a good cause.

The corrugated iron walls inside the bar are covered with signatures, phrases, messages and poems. For a small fee, which is donated to The Royal Flying Doctor Service, visitors can pen their own poetry or prose, if they can find a space. It's all good fun for a worthy cause.

The Tilpa Pub is a much talked about destination for those travelling along the Darling River between Bourke and Wilcannia.

Australian Bush Pubs | **235**

WARREGO HOTEL

Sitting by the Warrego River, the pub was constructed of mud bricks in 1913 and is thought to be the country's sole remaining licenced hotel built by this ancient method.

**Warrego Hotel
Albury Street, Fords Bridge
New South Wales
(02) 6874 7877**

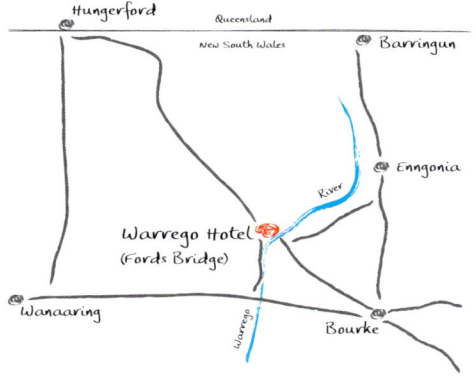

Along with being famous as home to Australia's last example of an operating mud brick pub, Fords Bridge is also known for its Warrego River yabbies, reputed far and wide as some of the tastiest in the outback.

Built in 1913, the current pub stands on the site of the old Salmon Ford Hotel, first licenced by Michael McAuliffe in the early 1870s. It is thought that before this time a sly grog shop would have operated at the nearby river crossing, servicing the coach route between Bourke and Hungerford.

The outback bard, Henry Lawson, passed this way in December 1892 on his epic walk from Bourke to Hungerford and back, calling in at the settlement's Salmon Ford pub to quench his ferocious thirst and see in the New Year.

Walk through the front door of the pub and you're cast straight into the spacious front room with its large wrap around bar. Most people take their drinks at the bar and there are plenty of stools to accommodate. Off to one side is a pot belly heater which keeps those chilly outback nights in check.

A door in the back wall of the bar opens into a large room sporting a pool table. It is from here that, if staying the night, you access the four guest rooms. Near the doorway some plaster has been removed from the wall, offering a glimpse of a section of the pub's sturdy adobe construction.

Fords Bridge is along the Dowling Track, a signposted 560km outback touring route linking Bourke in north-western New South Wales with Quilpie in Queensland.

Australian Bush Pubs

WILLIAM CREEK HOTEL

William Creek is one of the smallest towns in Australia and sits on the world's largest cattle station — the 24 000 square kilometre Anna Creek Station — which is almost half the size of Tasmania!

William Creek Hotel
Oodnadatta Track, William Creek
South Australia
(08) 8670 7880

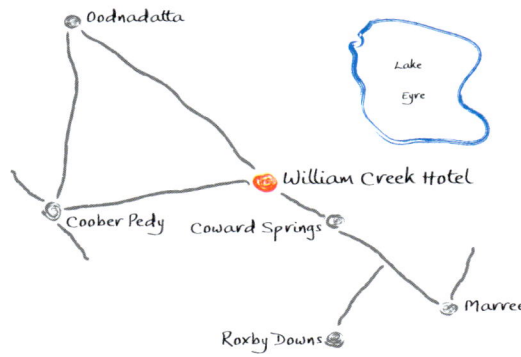

The hotel at William Creek is the only boozer on the Oodnadatta Track between Marree and Oodnadatta. Still largely in its original guise, the pub provides an insight into outback life and is filled, literally, to the rafters with unique mementos left over the years by tens of thousands of visitors. The rustic timber and corrugated iron building, dating from 1887, is like a visitors book. Over the years the walls have been covered with business cards, hand scrawled notes, bras, jocks and almost anything else which comes to hand.

William Creek was established along the Overland Telegraph Line and acted as a service point for both the line workers and camel strings operating along the route. When the railway reached here in 1885, it was seen as a vital watering and service point on the narrow-gauge line between Marree and Oodnadatta. The site had already been named in 1859 by explorer John McDouall Stuart after the second son of John Chambers, a pioneer pastoralist and a staunch supporter of Stuart's explorations.

The pub wasn't licenced as a hotel until 1935. Before this it was a boarding house, then became a store and, allegedly, an illegal wine bar.

The pub's painted corrugated iron walls reflect that unique character quintessential to bush pubs. With the closure of the hotel at Tarcoola, the William Creek Pub is the only corrugated iron hotel still trading in South Australia.

The pub's facade gives little indication of what awaits inside. Once through the enclosed screened verandah, there's the front bar and dining room

Australian Bush Pubs | 243

around the back, past the small pool room. The ornate — for a bush pub — front bar came from the Coward Springs Hotel, which was once situated further east down the track.

At the bar you're likely to meet locals from nearby cattle stations, fellow travellers exploring the Oodnadatta Track or heading to places further afield. There is also the constant flow of overseas tourists, many of them European backpackers who venture to this remote outpost to experience Australia's outback.

The Oodnadatta Track

The Oodnadatta Track passes through a mixture of plains and undulating countryside, running between Marree in the south and Marla on the Stuart Highway in the north. Largely following the route of the Old Ghan Railway, remnants and sidings of which feature prominently on the trip. Corrugations, potholes, loose stones, sand patches and lots of bulldust are constant companions, but in spite of this, it is generally passable to conventional vehicles. After rain, it is usually only suitable for four-wheel drives.

William Creek is located roughly one third the distance along the track from Marree.

The Old Ghan Railway Line was used for the last time in October 1980, but the William Creek Hotel is still serving travellers.

YARAKA HOTEL

The focal point for the small outback Queensland community, the Yaraka Hotel would have been a rip roaring joint back in the town's heyday of the 1920s when the railway came to town.

Yaraka Hotel
Jarley Street, Yaraka
Queensland
(07) 4657 5526

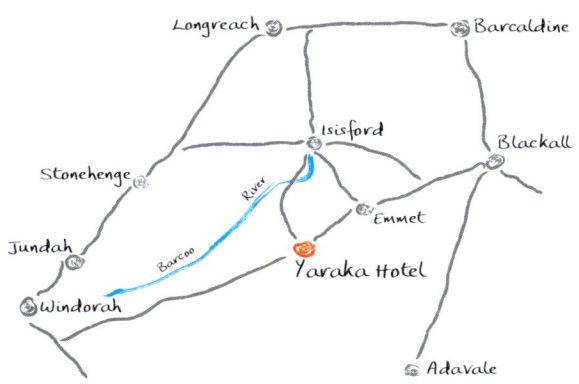

In 1910 work began on a 189 mile railway which would connect Blackall with Windorah, part of the Queensland Government's Great Western Railways Act. By 1917, after a number of delays, the line had reached Yaraka. It didn't go any further. Yaraka became 'the end of the line'.

At first Yaraka was a railway worker's camp, but during the 1920s through to the 1930s it gained an air of permanency with stores, boarding houses, garage and in 1923, a police station. The first Yaraka Hotel was a flash affair, being a two storey building which was moved from Mt Morgan by train. It was located where the present day church stands and was destroyed by fire.

The single storey timber and iron building which acts as the pub today was first licenced to Mick Bauer sometime in the early 1930s. Over the ensuing years the pub changed hands a number of times until it ceased trading in 1987. It stayed closed until 1989 when it reopened and has continued to trade since.

The Yaraka Hotel is a good, honest, and above all, friendly outback watering hole. It's neat and tidy and not plastered with paraphernalia found in many outback pubs these days. Inside there is a long bar with a dining area located off to one side. Out through the back door is a beer garden with a separate accommodation block off this.

Today the railway line is quiet. The last train ran to Yaraka in 2007.

INDEX

A

Ada's Veil 16
Adavale Pub 15, 16
adobe 236
Adelaide River Inn 18
Albert Hotel 23
Alice Springs 27, 131, 137, 139
Anna Creek Station 241
Archibald Prize 220
Auntie Barrett 87
Australian Consolidated Pastoral Co 160

B

Balonne River 154
Balranald 97, 98
Barrett, Emily 87
Barringun 53
Barrow Creek 27, 28
Barrow Creek Hotel 27, 28
Bathurst 199, 200
Bedourie 183, 184
Bedourie Camp Oven 184
beer-drinking pig 227
Bendoc 56
Berrima 208
Betoota Hotel 27
Birdsville 27, 35, 38, 137, 139
Birdsville Hotel 35
Birdsville Track 35, 137, 139
Birdum 61, 129, 131
Blackall 247
Blackwater Creek 15, 16
Bloomfield Track 132
Blue Heeler Hotel 41
bombed 131
bombing 61
border 51, 53, 56, 91, 107, 154, 188, 192
Boulia 141
Bourke 188, 192, 232, 235, 236
Broad Arrow 47, 48
Broad Arrow Tavern 47
Broken Hill 195, 196
Burke and Wills 97, 107, 108
Burketown 87
bushranger 91, 94, 170, 223

C

Cairns 167
camel 70, 139, 141, 241
Cameron Corner 51, 53
Cameron Corner Store 51
Cameron, John 53
Camooweal 87
Cape Tribulation 132
Captain Melville 223
Captain Moonlight 170
Captain Starlight 176
cattle 167, 176
cattle duffing 176
Central Australian Railway 137
Channel Country 38, 183
charcoal burners 97
Charleville 74
Charters Towers 146
Cheepie 203
Chillagoe 70
Chillagoe Smelters 70
Chinese 56, 187
Cloncurry 213
Cobb Co 15, 74, 91, 141, 176, 187, 188, 200, 203, 204, 208, 219
Cobdogla Station 170
cockies 232
Cogoon Station 163
collectibles 176
Combo Waterhole 41
Commercial Hotel 56
Cook, Nathaniel 110
Cooktown 132
Coongan River 110
Cooper Creek 107, 108, 160, 163
copper 68, 70
Copperfield 70
Copperfield Gorge 68
Copperfield River 68
Coward Springs Hotel 244
Cunnamulla 74, 188
Cunningham 146
curios 176
customs post 35, 91

D

Dagworth Station 41
Daintree Rainforest 132
Daintree, Richard 70
Daly Waters Pub 61, 62
Dargo Hotel 67
Darling River 232, 235
Darwin 129, 131
Delaney, Jim 102
Delegate River Tunnel 56
Depot Glen 24
Dig Tree 108
Dowdican, Michael 97
Dowling Track 236
drovers 35, 61, 129, 137, 141, 160, 170, 183, 213
droving 27, 107, 137, 139, 154, 184, 213, 232
Drysdale, Russell 219
Duck Creek 203
Duddy, Andrea Tom 176
Dunolly 223

E

Einasleigh 68, 70
Einasleigh Gorge 68
Einasleigh Hotel 68
Einasleigh Mine 70
Eromanga 187
Errinundra Plateau 56
Ethabuka Spring 183
Etheridge Railway 70
Euronghoola Creek 187

F

Falconio, Peter 28
fire 56, 67, 160, 180, 183, 195, 203, 219, 247
fireplace 41, 97, 183, 188, 227
Flinders Grass 176
Flowers, Brad & Nicole 170
Fords Bridge 236
Forsayth 70

INDEX

G

Gaffney's Creek 119
Garrett's Beerhouse 119
Georgina River 213
Georgina Stock Route 183, 213
Ghan Railway 139, 244
ghost 23, 68, 122, 170, 180
Gladstone Hotel 74
Glendambo 122, 127
Glengarry Hilton 78
gold 18, 23, 24, 48, 56, 67, 68, 84, 102, 110, 119, 151, 180, 199, 200, 219, 223
Golden Triangle 223
goldfield/s 23, 47, 67, 98, 110, 151, 200, 219, 223
Goulburn 151
Goulburn River 119
graffiti 235
Grand Hotel 83, 84
Grawin 79
grazier/s 110, 122, 141, 203, 223
Great War 83, 102
Great Western Hotel 15
Green Lizard Room 38
Gregory Downs Hotel 87
Gregory River 87
Grey Range 163
Guinness Book of Records 110
Gulf Savannah 70

H

Haken, Robbo 18
Harper, James 208
Hebel 91, 94
Hebel Hotel 91
Helenvale 132
Hergott Springs 137
Herrgott, David 137
Hilton 79
hitching posts/rails 91, 141
Hollywood 196
Homebush Hotel 97
Howitt, Alfred 108
Hughenden 167
Hume, Andrew 163
Hungerford 188, 192, 236
Huns Head 203

I

Imperial Hotel 102
Inglewood 223
Innamincka 107, 108, 139
Innamincka Hotel 107
Ironclad Hotel 110
Ivanhoe 97, 98

J

Jamieson 119
Jennacubbine Tavern 115
Jervis Bay 151

K

Kalgoorlie 48, 83
Kelly, Dan 91
Kennedy Developmental Road 167
Kennedy, Patrick 15
Kevington Hotel 118
Kevy 118
Kidman, Sidney 219
King, John 108
Kingoonya 122, 127
Kingoonya Hotel 122
Kookynie 83, 84
Kyabra 187, 203
Kynuna 41

L

Lake Eyre 139
Larrimah 129, 131
Larrimah Hotel 129
Lawn Hill National Park 87
Laws, John 47
Lawson, Henry 192, 236
Lees, Joanne 28
Leichhardt, Ludwig 163
Lightning Ridge 79, 94
Lions Den Hotel 132
Little Annan River 132
Logan 223
Lynd Junction 167

M

Macs Creek 119
Mad Max II 195, 196
Marble Bar 110
Marla 244
Marree 35, 137, 139, 183, 241, 244
Marree Hotel 137
McAuliffe, Michael 236
McNamara, Eileen 204
Melville Caves 223
memorabilia 27, 35, 62, 91, 132, 176, 188, 195
Mendel, Moritz 199, 200
Menindee 97
Menzies 48
Middleton Hotel 141
military 61, 129, 131
Miller, Max 219
Milo Welford Holdings 16
Milparinka 23, 24, 219
miners 24, 56, 67, 119, 187, 200, 203
Mingela Hotel 146
Moliagul 223
Monaro 151
Moonie River 154, 159
Morant, Harry, 232
Mt Isa 131, 213
Mt Morgan 247
mud brick 236
Mungindi 154, 159
Mungo National Park 97
Murdoch, Bradley John 28
Murray River 98, 87, 170
Murray River Cod 232
Murray, John 94
Murrumbidgee River 97

N

Nerriga Hotel 151
New Einasleigh Copper Mine 70
Newcastle Range 68
Nhall, Sandy 51
Nindigully Hotel 159
Nindigully Pub 154
Nindigully Station 154
Noccundra 160, 163
Noccundra Hotel 160
Nockatunga Station 160, 163
North Australia Railway 129
North Australian Hotel 146
Nowra 151

INDEX

O

Oasis Roadhouse 167
oil 51, 160
Old Ghan 137, 244
Oodnadatta 137, 139, 241
Oodnadatta Track 139, 241, 244
opal 79, 187, 203
Overland Corner Hotel 170
Overland Telegraph 61, 139, 241

P

Paroo River 188
Paterson, Banjo 41
Penarie 97, 98
pepper tree 98
Pilton, Les 28
Poole, James 24
Prairie Hotel 176, 180
prospector/s 23, 48, 67, 98, 110, 119, 151, 199, 223
pubobilia 27
Pugh, Clifton 219, 220
Pyengana 227, 231

Q

Queensland Legislative Council 16
Queensland Surveyor-General 16
Quilpie 15, 203, 236

R

railway 18, 48, 74, 83, 122, 127, 129, 137, 139, 146, 241, 244, 247
Ravenswood 102, 146
Ravenswood Junction 146
Razorback 196
Readford, Harry 176
Remienko, Seigmund 27
ringer/s 27, 35, 180
Riverina 98
rouseabouts 232
Royal Flying Doctor Service 235
Royal Hotel Bedourie 183
Royal Hotel Eromanga 187
Royal Hotel 183, 187, 199
Royal Mail Hotel 188

S

Salmon Ford Hotel 236
saltbush 98
savannah 167
savannahland 68
Savannahlander 70
shearers 23, 41, 51, 91, 97, 122, 223, 232
shearing 176
Shoalhaven River 151
Silverton Hotel 195, 196
Simpson Desert 35, 139
Siwers, Koss 16
sly grog 151, 199
Sofala Royal Hotel 199
South Western Hotel 203
squatters 176
St Columba Falls 227, 231
St Columba Falls Hotel 227
St George 91, 154, 159
Stevens, Ernst 16
stock route 35, 160, 183, 213
Stuart Highway 27, 28, 122, 129, 244
Stuart, John McDouall 61, 137, 241
Sturt, Charles 24
Surveyor General Inn 208

T

Tarcoola 241
Tasmanian Tiger 231
teamsters 151, 160
telegraph 18, 27, 61, 139, 241
Tennant Creek 27
Thargomindah 188, 203
The Central Hotel 68
The Dangi Pub 213
The Family Hotel 219
The Ghan 139
The Granites 24, 219
The Logan Pub 223
The Lynd Mine 70
The Old Ringer's Bar 180
The Pub in the Paddock 227
The Triangle 223
thylacine 231
Throssel, Captain Hugo 117
Tibooburra 24, 51, 53, 108, 160, 219, 220
Tilpa Hotel 232
Tilpa Pub 235
Tintinchilla Station 16

Todd, Charles 18
Toompine Pub 203
Townsville 146
Trans-Continental Railway 122, 127
traveller/s 23, 27, 35, 41, 51, 61, 62, 67, 87, 91, 97, 107, 119, 127, 132, 137, 139, 141, 154, 159, 160, 167, 176, 203, 219, 244
truckies 129, 141, 167
Tully, William Alcock 16
Turon River 199, 200

U

Urandangi Hotel 213

V

Victoria River 163
Victorian Exploring Expedition 108

W

Walgett 79, 91
Waltzing Matilda 41
Walwa 87
Warrego Hotel 236
Warrego River 74, 236
Warri Warri Gate 108
Watson brothers 87
Wedderburn 223
Welcome Stranger 223
Wilcannia 235
William Creek Hotel 241, 244
Williams, RM 41, 184
Williams, Sidney 129
Wilson River 160, 163
Windorah 247
Winton 141
World Heritage Listed 97, 132
World War I 84, 117, 137, 200
World War II 18, 20, 61
Wyandra 74

Y

yabbies 236
Yaraka Hotel 247

Z

Ziggy 27

Australian Bush Pubs | 253

In Memoriam

Farewell to these much-loved drinking holes. Featured in the previous edition of this book, they have since closed (in two cases sadly burnt down). Clockwise from top left: Grove Hill Hotel (Douglas-Daly NT), Espanol Hotel (Lappa Junction QLD), Tattersalls Hotel (Barringun NSW) and the Ora Banda Inn (Ora Banda WA).

About the Authors

Some would say that Craig Lewis and Cathy Savage quite enjoy the occasional beer and looking at the pages of this book they seem to spend a fair bit of time in pubs! But, of course, it's all in the name of research. Since the first edition of *Australian Bush Pubs* the pair have continued to travel extensively throughout the countryside in search of quirky hostelries, many of which they have luckily just stumbled upon, tucked away in the backblocks. Their quest to highlight an updated selection of Australia's best bush watering holes is presented in this new edition.

For over twenty years Craig and Cathy have been photographing and writing about the Australian bush — their travels having taken them across the length and breadth of Australia in search of new and interesting destinations. Bush pubs are just one of the many facets of Australia's remote parts which piques their interest. The pair have numerous guidebook and photobook titles to their credit, including the best-selling *Camping Guide to Australia* and the stunningly photographed *High Country Huts – A Celebration of Australia's Mountain Shelters*.

Craig and Cathy make their home on a small, secluded farm on the eastern Monaro region in southern New South Wales.

AUSTRALIAN BUSH PUBS

The authors and publisher acknowledge the Traditional Custodians of country throughout Australia and their connections to land, sea and community. We pay our respect to their Elders past, present and emerging.

Boiling Billy, a licensed imprint of
Woodslane Press
10 Apollo Place, Warriewood
NSW 2102 Australia
Tel: 02 8445 2300
Email: info@woodslane.com.au
www.woodslanepress.com.au

First published in Australia in 2009
Second edition published in Australia in 2016
This third edition published in Australia in 2023
Printed in China by Jilin GIGO

Copyright © concept, text and maps Craig Lewis and Cathy Savage 2009, 2016 & 2023 except where indicated below
Copyright © photographs Craig Lewis/Boiling Billy Images 2009, 2016 & 2023 except where indicated below

The following images are © and courtesy:
Pages 6 (top left photo), 170-175: Overland Corner Hotel; pages 6 (bottom left photo), 47: Broad Arrow Tavern; pages 6 (right hand three photos), 208-211 (inc. text): Simon Punch; pages 18-21 (inc. text): Louise Denton; pages 22-25 (except top right on p24): Albert Hotel; pages 30, 31, 32 (bottom right): Paul Makepeace; page 32 (top left): Ninderry Studios; page 32 (other photos) and text on pages 30-33: Betoota Hotel (Katrina Armanasco and Robert Haken); page 33: Rochelle Cains; pages 58, 59 (middle top and bottom, and top right): Commercial Hotel; pages 114-117 (inc. text): Erin Littlehill; pages 120 (except middle top), 121: Kevington Hotel; pages 202-205: South Western Hotel.

Design, and maps on pages 18, 31, 115 and 208 by Christine Schiedel

This publication is copyright. All rights reserved. No part of this publication may be reproduced, stored in a retrieval system, or transmitted by any form or by any means electronic, mechanical, photocopying, recording or otherwise, without the express written permission of the publisher.

Whilst all care has been taken by the authors and publisher to ensure that the information contained in this book is accurate and up-to-date, the authors nor the publisher can not take any responsibility for the information contained herein.

 A catalogue record for this book is available from the National Library of Australia

 MIX Paper from responsible sources FSC® C151165